THE
HOOVER
DAM

BUILDING
HISTORY
SERIES

THE HOOVER DAM

by Marcia Amidon Lüsted

LUCENT
BOOKS®

THOMSON
—————★—————™
GALE

San Diego • Detroit • New York • San Francisco • Cleveland
New Haven, Conn. • Waterville, Maine • London • Munich

For more information, contact
Lucent Books
27500 Drake Rd.
Farmington Hills, MI 48331-3535
Or you can visit our Internet site at http://www.gale.com

LIBRARY OF CONGRESS CATALOGING-IN-PUBLICATION DATA

Lüsted, Marcia Amidon.
   The Hoover Dam / by Marcia Amidon Lüsted.
p. cm. — (Building history series)
Includes bibliographical references and index.
   ISBN 1-59018-296-0 (hardback : alk. paper)
   1. Hoover Dam (Ariz. and Nev.)—History—Juvenile literature. I. Title. II. Series.
TC557.5.H6 L87 2003
   627'.82'0979313—dc21

                                               2002153399

Printed in the United States of America

CONTENTS

FOREWORD

Throughout history, as civilizations have evolved and prospered, each has produced unique buildings and architectural styles. Combining the need for both utility and artistic expression, a society's buildings, particularly its large-scale public structures, often reflect the individual character traits that distinguish it from other societies. In a very real sense, then, buildings express a society's values and unique characteristics in tangible form. As scholar Anita Abramovitz comments in her book *People and Spaces*, "Our ways of living and thinking—our habits, needs, fear of enemies, aspirations, materialistic concerns, and religious beliefs—have influenced the kinds of spaces that we build and that later surround and include us."

That specific types and styles of structures constitute an outward expression of the spirit of an individual people or era can be seen in the diverse ways that various societies have built palaces, fortresses, tombs, churches, government buildings, sports arenas, public works, and other such monuments. The ancient Greeks, for instance, were a supremely rational people who originated Western philosophy and science, including the atomic theory and the realization that the Earth is a sphere. Their public buildings, epitomized by Athens's magnificent Parthenon temple, were equally rational, emphasizing order, harmony, reason, and above all, restraint.

By contrast, the Romans, who conquered and absorbed the Greek lands, were a highly practical people preoccupied with acquiring and wielding power over others. The Romans greatly admired and readily copied elements of Greek architecture, but modified and adapted them to their own needs. "Roman genius was called into action by the enormous practical needs of a world empire," wrote historian Edith Hamilton. "Rome met them magnificently. Buildings tremendous, indomitable, amphitheaters where eighty thousand could watch a spectacle, baths where three thousand could bathe at the same time."

In medieval Europe, God heavily influenced and motivated the people, and religion permeated all aspects of society, molding people's worldviews and guiding their everyday actions. That spiritual mindset is reflected in the most important medieval structure—the Gothic cathedral—which, in a sense, was a model of heavenly cities. As scholar Anne Fremantle so elegantly phrases it, the cathedrals were "harmonious elevations of stone and glass reaching up to heaven to seek and receive the light [of God]."

Our more secular modern age, in contrast, is driven by the realities of a global economy, advanced technology, and mass communications. Responding to the needs of international trade and the growth of cities housing millions of people, today's builders construct engineering marvels, among them towering skyscrapers of steel and glass, mammoth marine canals, and huge and elaborate rapid transit systems, all of which would have left their ancestors, even the Romans, awestruck.

In examining some of humanity's greatest edifices, Lucent Books' Building History series recognizes this close relationship between a society's historical character and its buildings. Each volume in the series begins with a historical sketch of the people who erected the edifice, exploring their major achievements as well as the beliefs, customs, and societal needs that dictated the variety, functions, and styles of their buildings. A detailed explanation of how the selected structure was conceived, designed, and built, to the extent that this information is known, makes up the majority of the volume.

Each volume in the Lucent Building History series also includes several special features that are useful tools for additional research. A chronology of important dates gives students an overview, at a glance, of the evolution and use of the structure described. Sidebars create a broader context by adding further details on some of the architects, engineers, and construction tools, materials, and methods that made each structure a reality, as well as the social, political, and/or religious leaders and movements that inspired its creation. Useful maps help the reader locate the nations, cities, streets, and individual structures mentioned in the text; and numerous diagrams and pictures illustrate tools and devices that bring to life various stages of construction. Finally, each volume contains two bibliographies, one for student research, the other listing works the author consulted in compiling the book.

Taken as a whole, these volumes, covering diverse ancient and modern structures, constitute not only a valuable research tool, but also a tribute to the human spirit, a fascinating exploration of the dreams, skills, ingenuity, and dogged determination of the great peoples who shaped history.

Important Dates in the Building of the Hoover Dam

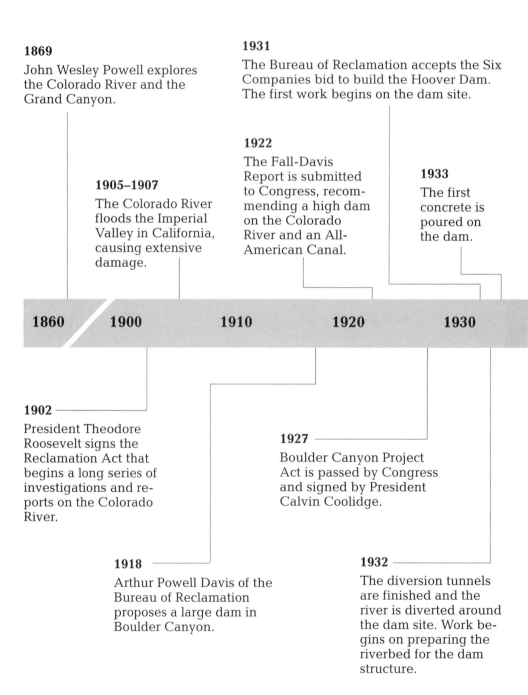

1869

John Wesley Powell explores the Colorado River and the Grand Canyon.

1931

The Bureau of Reclamation accepts the Six Companies bid to build the Hoover Dam. The first work begins on the dam site.

1922

The Fall-Davis Report is submitted to Congress, recommending a high dam on the Colorado River and an All-American Canal.

1905–1907

The Colorado River floods the Imperial Valley in California, causing extensive damage.

1933

The first concrete is poured on the dam.

1860   **1900**   **1910**   **1920**   **1930**

1902

President Theodore Roosevelt signs the Reclamation Act that begins a long series of investigations and reports on the Colorado River.

1927

Boulder Canyon Project Act is passed by Congress and signed by President Calvin Coolidge.

1918

Arthur Powell Davis of the Bureau of Reclamation proposes a large dam in Boulder Canyon.

1932

The diversion tunnels are finished and the river is diverted around the dam site. Work begins on preparing the riverbed for the dam structure.

1934

The construction of the All-American Canal begins.

1936

Generators in the dam's powerhouse begin generating electricity.

1939

Boulder Dam becomes the largest hydroelectric facility in the world, a distinction it holds until 1949.

1987

Hoover Dam celebrates its fiftieth anniversary, and the major cost of construction has now been repaid to the Federal Treasury. The dam is designated as a National Historic Landmark.

2001

A new visitors' center is constructed at the dam to handle the increasing number of tourists. The dam is again closed to all traffic after the September 11 bombing of the World Trade Center and the Pentagon.

| 1935 | 1940 | 1950 | 1980 | 2005 |

1935

Boulder Dam begins storing water in Lake Mead. The last concrete is poured on the dam, and President Franklin Roosevelt dedicates the structure.

1947

Congress officially renames Boulder Dam as Hoover Dam, in honor of president Herbert Hoover, ending years of name confusion.

2002

Traffic continues to be restricted throughout 2002.

1941

Boulder Dam closes to the public shortly after the Japanese bombing of Pearl Harbor, and remains restricted for the duration of World War II.

INTRODUCTION

WHY BUILD A DAM?

In 1985, the Hoover Dam celebrated its fiftieth anniversary. It is considered to be one of the greatest engineering achievements in American history. It was recognized in 1955 as one of the seven Modern Civil Engineering Wonders of the United States, named a National Historic Landmark in 1985, and listed in 1999 as one of the Top Ten Construction Achievements of the twentieth century. But beyond the facts of its sheer size and the magnitude of the construction project involved in its building, the Hoover Dam is credited with the creation of the modern American West. Without the dam, the huge cities of California and other western states would not have had the water necessary to make them what they are today.

LIFE BEFORE THE DAM

As early as the 1850s, Americans were exploring the Colorado River, on which the Hoover Dam is built, for its potential use in commerce. Many thought it could be used for transportation and for shipping goods and supplies, in the same way that the Mississippi and Missouri Rivers were used in the Midwest. The Colorado River was not easily navigated, however, because of its shifting currents, frequent rapids, and changing water levels. The river water carried huge amounts of silt as it carved out the canyons along its length. One of the slogans given to the Colorado River was that it was "too thick to drink and too thin to plow."[1] Early explorers declared the river to be profitless and unsuited for commerce.

In 1869 John Wesley Powell, a one-armed veteran of the Civil War, made a famous trip down the Colorado that finally mapped the river in its entirety. He agreed that the river had little value as a means of transportation, and the surrounding climate was so harsh that very little of it would be suitable farmland unless it were irrigated. He did not foresee that one day the technology would be available to alter geography and conform the climate to the needs of the huge agricultural farms of the modern West. Powell saw only a wild, unpredictable river, far too vast to be controlled by man.

The Colorado River flows through several canyons, including the Grand Canyon (pictured). Pioneers explored the river as early as the 1850s, but it was not fully mapped until 1869.

THE FIRST ATTEMPTS AT IRRIGATION

The Colorado River originates in the Rocky Mountains of north central Colorado and stretches fourteen hundred miles to the Gulf of California. It drains an area equal to one-twelfth the size of the United States. After flowing through a series of canyons, including the Grand Canyon, the river enters one of the hottest and driest areas of the United States as it runs between Arizona and California. Temperatures in this area can reach 125 degrees

Fahrenheit in the summer. However, this area was not always a dry desert. Once there was an ancient seabed here, called the Salton Sink, located below sea level. The early explorers of the river began to consider the possibility of digging an irrigation canal from the river into this area. There was a dry channel cut by the Colorado River during its flood stage, into the Alamo and New River channels of Mexico. From there gravity would bring the water into a newly built canal and then into California.

In 1901 the proposed canal was built from the Colorado River, running south and west into Mexico before turning north again and delivering water into what was renamed the Imperial Valley of California. This was thought to be a much more attractive name than the Salton Sink.

The canal was initially a huge success. Farmers poured into the Imperial Valley. By 1904 there were seven thousand people living there, and the agricultural production was even better than the original explorers had expected. The value of the crops produced in the valley had surpassed a million dollars, ten thousand cattle grazed in the area, and experimental crops of cotton and melons were flourishing. The Colorado River was to prove, however, that it was still wild and untamed. The canal itself was already filling in with silt deposited by the river when a series of floods in 1905 destroyed the flimsy control gates that regulated the flow of water into the valley. Soon the entire force of the flooding river flowed into the valley, destroying homes, railroads, and farmland and creating a thirty-mile-long lake at the bottom of the valley, appropriately named the Salton Sea.

The powerful rapids of the Colorado River caused early attempts to control its flow to fail.

It took eighteen months of continuous work building new levees, which were earthen embankments designed to prevent flooding, and the expenditure of over $2 million, to get the river back into its original course, only to have it flood again in 1906. This taught the farmers and engineers valuable lessons about trying to alter the natural course of the wild Colorado River, and westerners began to demand a more lasting solution to river control. They wanted a permanent dam on the Colorado.

THE PURPOSE OF A DAM

There were three major reasons for building a high, permanent dam on the Colorado River. The first was irrigation and water supply, as illustrated by the earlier disastrous attempts in the Imperial Valley. The deserts of the American West needed water to become farmland, and the growing cities of California needed water for their inhabitants. Along with supplying water, a dam was also needed to control the river during times of flooding or during low water cycles. A dam would regulate the flow of water, holding it back when the river flooded, and pooling it in a reservoir for those times when the water level was low and more needed to be released. A reservoir would also control the loads of silt that the river carried, allowing it to sink to the lake bed instead of being deposited downriver to clog irrigation canals. The third reason was the need for electrical power. A large dam could generate hydroelectric power by using the flow of water to operate huge generators, and the American West was just as hungry for electricity as it was for water. Electricity could also be sold as a way to recover the initial cost of building the dam.

With all these factors in mind, Congress ordered the United States Department of the Interior to make an extensive survey of the entire Colorado River. They would then create a plan for a system of river controls, involving a series of dams, canals, and water storage. This was the first step in the process that would result in the eventual construction of the Hoover Dam.

FROM IDEA TO
CONSTRUCTION

Finding a solution to the water needs of the West and the control of the Colorado River was not going to be fast or simple. The Imperial Valley had already proven how dangerous it was to act on a plan for irrigation without looking at the larger issues of river control. Any project undertaken on the Colorado would need extensive study and planning before any sort of construction could begin, a process that would take years of research and government approval.

THE FALL-DAVIS REPORT

After the disastrous attempts at irrigating California's Imperial Valley, a bill was introduced into Congress for the construction of an All-American Canal. This would be a canal that would run entirely through United States land without detouring into Mexican territory. Having sections of the canal in Mexican territory, made it subject to the whims of local Mexican authorities, who often created difficulties for the crews who crossed the border to maintain and repair the irrigation system. Surprisingly, this bill was vetoed largely because of the efforts of Arthur Powell Davis, director of the United States Reclamation Service and the nephew of John Wesley Powell, who had originally explored the length of the Colorado River. It was assumed that Davis should have been in favor of any bill that would bring improvements to the water situation in the area, but Davis wanted to find a lasting solution and not just another project of limited value like the original Imperial Valley canal had been. He firmly believed that the only way to successfully irrigate the West was through a larger comprehensive plan that took into account the present and future needs of the entire area. Davis spoke of this as including "the construction of the interlocking network of dams, hydroelectric plants, aqueducts, and canals that would blunt the river's destructiveness and distribute its benevolence."[2]

Congress agreed with Arthur Powell Davis and commissioned an extensive study of the situation. River exploration had been taking place since 1902, as government geologists and hydrologists explored potential dam sites on the lower Colorado River. They speculated about how suitable the rock formations were in various canyons and made more precise calculations as the idea of building a dam took shape. Eight sites were first identified as being possible locations for a dam, but gradually these were narrowed down to two: Boulder Canyon and Black Canyon, both on the southeast tip of Nevada.

A report, consisting of hundreds of pages, including profiles of the river as well as the geological contents of the canyons, was drawn up. This study, called the Fall-Davis report, was issued in 1922. It made the recommendation that the United States build a dam at or near Boulder Canyon, which at the time was considered to be a better site than Black Canyon. The dam would then be the center of a new system of water storage and distribution.

Before the dam could become a reality, it was necessary to decide how the river's water would be distributed among the seven states involved. States that had a claim on potential irrigation and drinking water were Wyoming, Colorado, New Mexico, Utah, Nevada, Arizona, and California. Each state argued about how much water they felt they were entitled to, but no one could decide how to allocate the water fairly. A series of conferences took place, and those involved attempted to come to an agreement between the states, but no decision could be made. The government's representative at these conferences was Herbert Hoover, who at the time was the secretary of commerce under President Warren Harding. His compromise finally brought a halt to the water distribution arguments. The seven states were divided into two parts: the Upper Division (Wyoming, Colorado, Utah, and New Mexico) and the Lower Division (Nevada, California, and Arizona). Each division would receive 7.5 million acre-feet of water (an acre-foot is the amount of water needed to cover an acre of land one foot deep in water), which the individual states could divide among themselves at a later

U.S. secretary of commerce Herbert Hoover presides over a hearing to determine how the water of the Colorado River is to be apportioned. The meeting resulted in the Colorado River Compact.

date. This resulted in the Colorado River Compact, which was signed on November 24, 1922, and ratified by the individual states' legislatures. Arizona was the only state that never adopted the compact, but it was overruled because six out of the seven states did approve it.

But before Congress could approve the final funding necessary for constructing a dam, the exact location had to be pinpointed, and this would involve further exploration and study of the Colorado River area.

THE FINAL PREPARATIONS

There were three important criteria to be considered in finding a site for the dam. The first was the geological and topographical nature of the site. The rock in the canyon walls and riverbed had to be strong and stable, without cracks or faults, and the sand and gravel deposits in the riverbed could not be too deep because they would have to be excavated to reach bedrock on which to build the dam's foundations. This would require precise measurements both near and in the river.

The second criterion was the location of the potential reservoir behind the dam and how much water and river silt it would be capable of holding. It was necessary to have enough space for a sizeable reservoir, deep enough to hold water and trap silt without filling up too quickly over time.

The third criterion was the location of the site in relation to railroads and electrical power lines. A railroad was essential for

COLORADO RIVER BOATS

Even though John Wesley Powell had surveyed parts of the Colorado River during his explorations in the late 1860s and early 1870s, nearly eight hundred miles remained unsurveyed and uncharted by the 1920s, when the decision was made to find a site for a dam.

In order to make the difficult journey down the river possible, special boats were built, designed to withstand the wear and tear of the river's turbulence. Four eighteen-foot wooden boats were built in 1921. The boats resembled kayaks in their shape and they were made out of oak, spruce, and cedar wood. They had watertight compartments in the front and back to keep them afloat if they overturned.

During the explorations of the river, the surveyors often encountered rapids that were not marked on any charts or maps. The boatmen would turn the boats around and meet the rapids backward, rowing against the current to slow the boat down and minimize any damage from hitting rocks or other submerged obstacles.

Often the boatmen would steer the boats on the river while the engineers walked along the shore, gathering data on the rocks and canyon walls. At other times, the men would have to carry the boats around shallows because of seasonally low water.

One of these four survey boats, the *Marble*, is now on display in the museum at the Hoover Dam Visitor's Center.

transporting building materials to the dam site, and power would be needed for lighting and construction equipment. If the site were too remote, both of these vital services would be more costly and time consuming to construct.

Determining the best site would require an even more extensive exploration of the river and of both Boulder Canyon and Black Canyon, which had already been decided upon as the two most likely locations.

EXAMINING THE RIVER

Full-scale canyon testing would not be an easy task for the Bureau of Reclamation. The river was unstable and difficult to navigate, and trying to keep a boat in one position was nearly impossible. Some of the information needed could be gathered onshore by visually examining the two canyons, but most of it would require drilling deep into the canyon walls and the riverbed and extracting core samples of the rock. In his book *Hoover Dam: An American Adventure*, Joseph E. Stevens describes the process:

> Attempting to rig stable drilling platforms on the Colorado [River] was like trying to balance a tray of glasses on the rump of an angry saddle bronc. Outboard motors could not hold boats in position because of the river's fractious currents, which rose and fell, curved and swirled, surged and slackened with alarming unpredictability. There was only one way to set up a work station: drive ring bolts into the canyon walls, string steel cables across the river, and anchor wooden barges to the cables. . . . Fastened to the deck of each barge was a timber derrick from which hung a drill tipped with a diamond bit. When everything was ready, a ten-horsepower gasoline engine at the base of the derrick sputtered to life, the drill was lowered, and the rotating bit chewed into the river bottom. Samples were withdrawn from holes as deep as 200 feet.[3]

Topographical survey teams were also climbing the sheer canyon walls in order to accurately measure and map the area. Because of the steepness of the walls, shallow caves, and flaking rock that easily came loose, it was necessary to hack shallow trails, use ladders precariously lashed together, and to rig ropes and safety lines like those used by mountain climbers, for workers to hang from and swing into areas that were otherwise unreachable.

After two years of extensive work mapping and drilling the two canyons, the Reclamation Service finished its evaluation of potential sites in April 1923. Despite the earlier belief that Boulder Canyon was the best site, in the end it was Black Canyon that was selected as the best place to construct the dam. Its bedrock was more stable, there was less silt and debris on the riverbed, and the river's gap within the canyon was narrower, which would require less concrete and a smaller dam structure. It was also close to the town of Las Vegas and had easier access to the railroad. And so Black Canyon became the official site for

Surveyors assess the proposed dam site of Black Canyon. Although the Black Canyon site was chosen, the dam continued to be referred to as the Boulder Dam.

the new dam. Now that a site was chosen and the necessary measurements and investigations had taken place, the final push could be made in Congress for funding.

THE BOULDER CANYON PROJECT ACT

In 1924, the Bureau of Reclamation submitted an eight-volume report on Black Canyon, including tentative plans for the dam and the first cost estimates, to the Secretary of the Interior. Even though the project would now be located in Black Canyon, the dam had become known as the Boulder Canyon Dam and the name stuck in popular usage. The report, with its two thousand pages of facts and figures, was favorably received by the secretary and by those in Congress who supported the Colorado River development project. The next step would be formal approval from Congress.

Congressman Phil Swing and Senator Hiram Johnson had introduced the first bill, called the Swing-Johnson bill, to authorize construction in 1923. The fourth revision of this bill was introduced to Congress in December 1927. Despite a great deal of opposition from eastern politicians who did not see any benefit to their areas from a western dam project, the bill was passed on December 14—and signed into law by President Calvin Coolidge a week later. The final details of the Colorado River Compact, including dividing the water between the states involved, were also worked out. On June 25, 1929, the new president, Herbert Hoover, signed a proclamation authorizing the expenditure of $165 million to build the Boulder Dam and the All-American Canal. It had taken over five years of study, exploration, and political persuasion to lay the groundwork for the huge project.

CREATING A GIANT BLUEPRINT

While politicians were still arguing the Swing-Johnson bill and the merits of the Boulder Dam, government engineers were busy researching dam types. The Boulder Dam was to be a concrete arched-gravity dam. This design was dictated by the size and strength of the river and was seen as the only design possible for an undertaking of this size. The enormous weight and power of the blocked river water pushing against a flat-walled dam would have destroyed it in no time. The Boulder Dam would be curved or arched. With this shape, the force of the water would push into the curved concrete and naturally deflect into the canyon walls. The dam would also be triangular in cross section, with enormous thickness located at the base where the force of water is the greatest. The weight of the dam pressing into the canyon floor would be so great that in reality the arched wall was probably not even necessary, but it added more strength to the structure and also gave a visual impression of that strength to the eye of an observer.

Once the type of dam had been determined, more than thirty different design plans were drawn up by the Bureau of Reclamation design staff and extensively tested. Hundreds of

Designers and engineers assemble a model of Boulder Dam. Models were used to conduct stress tests to ensure that the actual dam could contain the Colorado River.

drawings were made, as well as huge rubber and plaster models that could be subjected to stress tests in laboratories, as described in a government pamphlet on the construction of the dam:

> Designs for all features were made in the Denver, Colorado office of the Bureau of Reclamation, and were complete down to the last nut and bolt. Models of structures were made to a scale as large as 1 to 20, research was conducted in many Universities, concrete cylinders as large as 3 feet in diameter were broken to ascertain the strength of the cobble-contained concrete. More than 400 separate drawings [were] on file in the Boulder City office.[4]

Finally the bureau design staff, led by chief engineer Raymond Walter and chief design engineer Jack Savage, decided on the final design for the Boulder Dam: a gigantic concrete wedge 727 feet high (as tall as a sixty-story skyscraper), 660 feet thick at the base but just 45 feet thick at the top. The design was declared to be safe and was accepted by a board of consulting engineers that had been appointed to monitor the design effort.

Accompanying the dam would be various other structures, including towers, tunnels, and cofferdams to temporarily hold back the flow of the river during construction. There would also be two huge spillways to release water from the reservoir during times of flooding, and a horseshoe-shaped powerhouse built at the base of the dam to produce electricity from the flow of water. The allocation of this electricity would also have to be agreed upon by the states and cities involved. Agreements were hammered out between the city of Los Angeles, the California Metropolitan Water District, the Southern California Edison Company, and the states of Nevada and Arizona, all of whom wanted to purchase shares of the water and electricity to be produced by the dam. This would guarantee a future income to the government to help repay the cost of building the dam.

As soon as funding had been approved for the dam, the first and most important step in construction took place as workers began to lay railroad track between Las Vegas and Black Canyon. Two and a half million dollars were earmarked for railroad construction. The Union Pacific Railroad would lay twenty-three miles of track from a junction south of Las Vegas

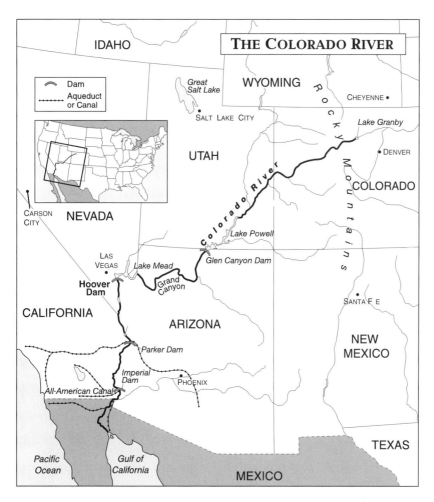

THE COLORADO RIVER

IDAHO

Dam
Aqueduct
or Canal

Great
Salt Lake

WYOMING

CHEYENNE •

SALT LAKE CITY

Lake Granby

UTAH

• DENVER

COLORADO

Colorado River

CARSON
CITY

NEVADA

Lake Powell

Glen Canyon Dam

LAS
VEGAS

Lake Mead

Grand
Canyon

Hoover
Dam

SANTA FE

CALIFORNIA

ARIZONA

NEW
MEXICO

Parker Dam

Imperial
Dam

PHOENIX

All-American Canal

TEXAS

Pacific
Ocean

Gulf of
California

MEXICO

Rocky Mountains

to the site selected for the future Boulder City, the yet-to-be-built town to house the dam workers. Switchyards, sidings, and repair shops would be built there, and then the government would be responsible for laying another ten miles of track to the rim of Black Canyon. From there, the contractor selected to build the dam would have to run the remaining tracks into the canyon itself. Crews began work in September 1930, and the governor of Nevada and the Department of the Interior decided that the occasion would be perfect for celebrating the project's official start-up. On September 17, 1930, a state holiday was declared and Secretary of the Interior Ray Lyman Wilbur and a crowd of dignitaries and onlookers stood in the 103-degree Nevada heat as Wilbur drove a silver railroad spike into the first rail. He made a short speech and concluded by saying, "I have the honor to name this greatest project of all time—the Hoover Dam."[5] This surprise renaming of the dam would only add to the confusion over its name, which would go on for years as it went back and forth between Hoover Dam and Boulder Dam.

The design for the dam was now in place. It had a new name, even if it was an unpopular one, an assured future income, and railroad access. It was time to find someone to build it.

NAME CONFUSION

One of the most confusing aspects of the history of Hoover Dam is the dam's name. After the initial exploration of the Colorado and its canyons indicated that Boulder Canyon would be the best site for the dam, the political name for the project became the Boulder Canyon Project and eventually the Boulder Canyon Act. When Black Canyon was ultimately chosen for the dam's location, the name Boulder Dam had already stuck in the media and the public mind so it continued to be used.

When Secretary of the Interior Ray Lyman Wilbur dedicated the railway built to the dam site in 1930, he announced that the dam would be named Hoover Dam, in honor of President Hoover and his efforts on behalf of the dam's construction. Many people were unhappy with this name change, believing that a dam should not be named after a president who was still in office. When Hoover lost the next presidential election to Franklin Roosevelt, the new secretary, Harold Ickes, decisively reinstated the name Boulder Dam. He claimed that Secretary Wilbur had acted improperly by naming the dam after Hoover because he had not had congressional authorization, and that the dam had already been known as Boulder Dam. The name stayed in place until 1947, when Congress officially voted to return the dam's name to Hoover Dam, again recognizing President Hoover's important role in the dam project. Many older reference books, movies, and even cartoons still refer to the dam as Boulder Dam, and the confusion continues today.

BIDDING ON THE DAM

The construction of the Hoover Dam would be the biggest construction contract in American history, and as the Depression hit America and times grew worse for most companies, the idea of landing such a huge contract was enticing. For five dollars a copy, potential construction companies could buy a booklet one hundred pages long that contained twenty-six drawings detailing the project, a timetable imposed by the government for the completion of the project, and the requirements for building a small city to house the dam workers, which would be called Boulder City. Contractors would bid on the job by submitting in writing the dollar amount for which they felt they could build the dam, and the company with the lowest price would win the job. This system of bidding was tricky in that a company had to allow enough money in their bid to make a profit from the construction, and yet not be underbid by another company.

In addition to bidding on the construction with a dollar amount, each company had to submit a $2 million bid bond and a $5 million performance bond. A bid bond was an amount of money submitted to the government at the time of bidding, guaranteeing the good faith of that company and that they would enter into the contract and have the necessary money to begin the project if awarded the job. A performance bond was posted once the contract was awarded and guaranteed that the construction company would complete the terms of the contract. This kind of money was unavailable to most construction companies, especially as the Depression grew worse.

The winning bid was submitted by a company that was actually a collection of six smaller companies. They came together to pool their resources for posting the bonds and completing the project. They called themselves, appropriately enough, Six Companies, and on March 4, 1931, in a smoky Bureau of Reclamation office in Denver, Colorado, Six Companies submitted the winning bid. It would construct the Hoover Dam and its accompanying structures for $448,890,955. The biggest engineering project so far in American history was about to begin.

THE PARTS OF A DAM

Six Companies had won the bidding for the Hoover Dam, but it was not as simple as just building a concrete dam in the middle of the Colorado River. As part of the future dam, Six Companies

SIX COMPANIES

Six Companies was created because of the need to raise the extraordinary amount of cash, $7 million, that was necessary to bid on the contract for building Hoover Dam. Six Companies was just as its name implied: six smaller companies that came together through mutual acquaintance to pool their resources and act as one company.

Raymond Walter, chief engineer of the Bureau of Reclamation, signs a contract awarding the Hoover Dam Project to Six Companies.

The companies were the Utah Construction Company of Ogden, Utah; the Morrison-Knudsen Company of Boise, Idaho; the J.F. Shea Company of Portland, Oregon; the Pacific Bridge Company, also of Portland, Oregon; MacDonald and Kahn Construction Company of San Francisco, California; and the Kaiser Paving Company of Oakland, California. In February 1931, the officials of these companies met in the Engineer's Club in San Francisco to work out the details of a partnership, including the amount of the bid for the Hoover Dam project and how they would finance the job. Six Companies was incorporated as a company on February 19, 1931.

Working together was not without difficulties. There were conflicting personalities among the strong leaders of each smaller company, most of whom had started their companies and had run them personally. Once Six Companies won the bid to build the dam, Chief Engineer Frank Crowe had to deal with the meddling of all the directors in every aspect of construction, often issuing conflicting instructions and wasting enormous amounts of time. Finally he appealed to the group to form a chain of command, and a four-man executive committee in charge of the details of the project was established.

Six Companies went on to build even more projects after Hoover Dam was finished, and became a leader in industrial and heavy construction. They were involved in oil refineries, shipbuilding, and government construction, as well as other dams.

would have to construct a series of buildings and tunnels necessary for the construction, and later for the maintenance of the Hoover Dam. The dam would have two intake towers that would rise from the waters of the future reservoir, where the lake water would enter the dam and be used to power the turbines that generate electricity. This would involve a series of tunnels blasted through the solid rock of the canyon walls. There would also be two spillways, used to release water into the tunnels in times of flooding when the reservoir's level grew too high and there was a threat of water flowing over the dam structure.

Located below the dam itself would be the power plant, where the river water would be used to turn turbines and create electricity. The outlet gates, which controlled any overflow from the spillways, would also be located in the canyon walls downstream from the dam.

The tunnels that would provide water to the power plants and carry it away from the intake towers and spillways would originate in four diversion tunnels, which would be constructed first to temporarily carry the Colorado River around the dam site so that the dam structure could be built on solid, dry bedrock. Blasting these tunnels would be the first major part of the dam's construction.

BOULDER CITY

The other large construction project involved in the whole Hoover Dam undertaking would be the building of Boulder City. This was a new plan incorporated into the project by the government, in which workers and their families would have proper housing instead of the traditional temporary construction camps. This plan was made necessary by the extreme conditions found near the dam site, where heat and the desert environment would take a high toll on workers.

Bureau of Reclamation commissioner Elwood Mead explained why Boulder City had been planned, in a speech he gave in January 1931:

> The summer wind which sweeps over the gorge from the desert feels like a blast from a furnace. How to overcome this and provide for the health and welfare of the workers has had much attention. The sun beats down on a

FRANK T. CROWE

One of the most important people associated with the building of the Hoover Dam was Frank T. Crowe, who was hired by Six Companies as chief engineer and supervisor of construction on the project. He was largely responsible for bringing the Hoover Dam project to an early and successful completion, even though his push to meet or even exceed the government's deadlines for certain stages of construction earned him the nickname Hurry-Up Crowe among the men who worked for him.

Crowe built six dams before the Hoover Dam, first as an engineer for the U.S. Bureau of Reclamation, and then as an engineer for the Morrison-Knudsen construction firm, one of the companies that eventually became part of Six Companies. He was known for his ability to solve problems as well as his knack for dealing fairly with his workers, many of whom followed him from job site to job site, affectionately calling him the Old Man.

When he was young, Crowe had traveled through the Colorado River canyons with Arthur Powell Davis, and he knew that a great dam would be built there one day. In his book *Great Projects*, James Tobin quotes Crowe's words about the Hoover Dam project: "I was wild to build this dam. I had spent my life in the river bottoms, and it meant a wonderful climax—the biggest dam ever built by anyone anywhere."

Crowe's dedication to the construction of the dam was apparent to everyone who worked for him. Bob Parker, a worker on the dam quoted in *Building Hoover Dam: An Oral History of the Great Depression* by Andrew J. Dunar and Dennis McBride, remembers: "Everyone who worked down here knew who Frank Crowe was. He was all over the job. His workmen, he knew them by their first name, nearly every one of them. Even we who did not work [directly] for him, he knew who we were. . . . But he never forgot you if you ever crossed him."

Crowe also had a good reputation with the larger community of construction companies and people. He pioneered new techniques, such as the cable system for overhead delivery of buckets of concrete, used on the Hoover Dam, and another pipe grid system for transporting cement.

The Hoover Dam was Frank Crowe's crowning achievement. He built more dams after "Hoover," but nothing as impressive. In 1945, following World War II, the U.S. government asked him to organize and direct the reconstruction work being done in Germany, but his doctor would not permit him to accept the job because of Crowe's failing health. He died on February 26, 1946, in California.

broken surface of lava rocks. At midday they cannot be touched with the naked hand. It is bad enough as a place for men at work. It is no place for a boarding house or a sleeping porch. Comfortable living conditions had to be found elsewhere.[6]

Boulder City was planned as a model city, where there would be none of the saloons and casinos of nearby Las Vegas. There would be a few permanent buildings, such as the offices of the Bureau of Reclamation and Six Companies, government lodges, and guest houses. There would be a rail yard and a business district, as well as machine shops and other necessary maintenance buildings for the dam.

The rest of Boulder City was intended to be temporary, existing just for the six years allotted for the construction of the dam. This included dormitories and a mess hall as well as small houses for workers and their families to rent cheaply.

READY TO BEGIN

Hoover Dam now had its contractor, and Six Companies had hired the man who would be one of the most important factors in the success of the entire construction project. His name was Frank Crowe, and among the group of construction workers in the West at that time, he already had a reputation for hard work and dedication and the ability to bring difficult projects to completion on schedule and within budget. Frank Crowe would be the biggest asset that Six Companies had as it began to work in Black Canyon.

GETTING STARTED

Once Six Companies was awarded the contract for the Hoover Dam project, it began to make preparations for the construction of the railroads and access roads that would bring materials and workers to Black Canyon. News of the dam construction and the thousands of jobs it would produce spread through the country like wildfire. Because of the Great Depression, which began with the stock market crash of 1929 and worsened steadily into the 1930s, one quarter of all Americans were jobless. Banks had failed and families lost their life savings. Desperate and homeless, they heard the news of the giant dam construction project in Nevada and started streaming toward Las Vegas in 1930, long before actual construction was set to begin. Las Vegas, however, was unprepared for the huge number of people and quickly became overwhelmed.

THE LAS VEGAS INVASION

Las Vegas in 1930 was a sleepy little town with five thousand residents, but as the unemployed flocked there in hopes of jobs on the dam, the town swelled with another ten thousand to twenty thousand newcomers. Leo Dunbar, who lived in Las Vegas at the time, describes the invasion in an oral history of the Hoover Dam construction:

> You've got to realize that when people found out that the project was going to be built, they flocked in here from all parts of the United States. This was the Great Depression, the period of 1928 to 1932 or '33. The fact that there was going to be work here induced people to

30

Crowds of people walk the streets of New York after the stock market crash of 1929. As word of the Hoover Dam project spread, people from all over the United States flocked to Las Vegas in hopes of finding work.

come in here—not only the men, but their families came with them. They just picked up whatever they had and loaded it into a truck and drove here, and had hopes of getting a job. There had been thousands of people that had moved in here. They had moved down on the river; they had moved into where Boulder City was supposed to be.[7]

Families camped in the square near Las Vegas's Union Station railroad station and all along the nearby roads in the extreme heat and dust of what was essentially a desert. Camps turned into small villages of people living in huts, shanties, or their cars, trying to escape the heat and waiting for the jobs to

LIVING IN THE DESERT

As hopeful families streamed into Las Vegas seeking employment on the dam, they found themselves living in harsh desert conditions. One of the temporary towns that sprang up was called Ragtown because so many of the houses were made of rags or cardboard. In Ragtown, or Hell's Hole as it was also called, families set up makeshift camps, sleeping in their cars, tents, or homemade shelters. This shantytown was home to more than a thousand men, women, and children in the summer of 1931, which was one of the hottest summers on record, even for the deserts of Nevada. There were no modern conveniences: Families drank river water and cooked over open campfires. There was no refrigeration or electricity and people used the river for bathing, or simply to sit in when the temperatures were unbearable.

In their book *Building Hoover Dam: An Oral History of the Great Depression*, authors Andrew Dunar and Dennis McBride interviewed hundreds of people who were involved with the construction of the dam. Erma Godbey, whose husband came to work at the dam, describes life in Ragtown: "We got ahold of some clothesline, and we had some safety pins. We put some poles in the ground and pinned . . . blankets with safety pins to these poles to try to make a little bit of shade from the terrible heat. It would get to be 120 by nine in the morning, and it wouldn't get below 120 before nine at night. I would wrap my babies in wet sheets so they could sleep."

What finally convinced Erma and her husband to leave Ragtown were the deaths of four women in one day from heat and illness. Other families had no choice and remained in Ragtown until Boulder City was finished and ready to house the dam workers in a safer environment.

begin. One of these towns was called McKeeversville, which had grown from a government tent camp for the project surveyors. Another town, first called Williamsville but later nicknamed Ragtown because most of the dwellings were made of rags or scrap cardboard, sprung up on the floodplain of the Colorado River and swelled to five hundred people.

Because of the overwhelming number of job seekers living in the terrible conditions of the desert, President Hoover ordered work to begin on the dam six months ahead of schedule. Facilities had not yet been built for the workers, and Boulder City was still just a design on paper, but the Hoover Dam was about to become a reality, and hiring workers would begin.

FINDING THE WORKERS

In 1930, the U.S. Department of Labor opened an employment office in a one-room wooden building in Las Vegas, run by a man named Leonard Blood and with the help of just one secretary. By the time word had gotten out about the imminent start of the dam construction, this tiny office had received twelve thousand letters of inquiry from all over the country, and twenty-four hundred employment applications had been filed, all for an eventual peak employment of only five thousand workers.

The wages for the workers on the Hoover Dam, while small in comparison to today's wages, were a tremendous enticement to men made jobless by the Depression. Pay ranged from fifty cents to $1.25 per hour, roughly $1,500 a year, a good amount of money at that time, especially for families who did not have enough to eat and were living in their cars.

Hiring began in 1931. Every time Frank Crowe came to Ragtown on his way up the river to the dam site by boat, hordes of desperate men surrounded him, pleading for jobs. Unfortunately, the first workers needed for the dam's construction had to be skilled and experienced at what they did. Word went out through all the construction camps of the West that Crowe was beginning another dam project and needed good workers. Many of these men had worked with Crowe on previous projects and dams, and these men formed the basis for the Hoover Dam builders. They were experienced miners, powder (explosive) men, tunnel men, engineers, and power shovel operators. These men would be the first to work in Black Canyon and prepare for the construction of the actual dam.

GETTING INTO THE CANYON

Crowe's men would be responsible for creating access to the canyon, which was necessary before any other work could begin. Black Canyon was not an easy place to work. The walls were sheer cliffs with no toeholds for climbing, and above the canyon on the rim there was nothing but naked desert. The first and most important step would be to blast access roads and railroad beds from these sheer walls so that the real work could begin with the most efficiency.

At this stage of the project, barges and launch boats began carrying men back and forth across the river, which was expensive and clumsy. Because of this, men with jackhammers pounded away at the canyon walls, creating roadbeds for vehicles and train tracks for better access to the site and making space for the two concrete-mixing plants that would also have

A four-ton dynamite blast detonates in Black Canyon. Dynamite was used to blast through canyon walls so access roads could be built.

to be built along the river. Dynamite was also used to blast into the walls, and in May 1931 one of the first accidents at the site took place when a blast two hundred feet overhead injured men working at river level, showering them with rock fragments. But explosives were not the biggest threat to the workers in the canyon. Although it was still early in the project, another condition was responsible for a far greater loss of life.

THE LONG SCORCHING SUMMER

The greatest obstacle for the men working in Black Canyon that summer was the heat. With temperatures routinely soaring over 110 degrees Fahrenheit and the black walls of the canyon intensifying the heat, men were falling victim to heat exhaustion, heatstroke, and dehydration. Symptoms included vomiting, convulsions, loss of consciousness, and elevated body temperature. As the working conditions worsened in the canyon, the number of men in the workforce was steadily increasing as access to the canyon improved and workers could begin on other construction tasks.

This led to more and more incidents of heat-related illness. The men were living in a series of wooden dormitories built on the riverbank, called River Camp, without air-conditioning, fans, or cold drinking water. It was eventually determined that many of them were not drinking enough water. Coupled with the relentless heat, the result was twenty deaths from heat prostration by the end of July, approximately one death every two days. If a worker collapsed, he would be packed in ice in an attempt to bring down his body temperature, but for many it was often too late. The sound of an ambulance arriving at the work site became as common as the sound of drilling.

The heat also made the workers lethargic and unproductive. If they wanted to keep their rigid construction schedule and complete each stage on time, Six Companies knew that it would have to provide better conditions, such as cooler dormitories to sleep in and cold water to drink, for their men. The company executives claimed that the president's decree that work begin a year early had left them no time to finish Boulder City and get the workers and families out of Ragtown and similar camps. From the workers' perspective, however, it seemed as if the company was putting the deadlines of the dam project ahead of the safety of its employees.

LIFE AT RIVER CAMP

The heat affected the men in company-built housing, just as it affected their families in Ragtown and other makeshift settlements. Terrible living conditions existed at River Camp, six two-story barracks built for workers on the river-bank at the entrance to Black Canyon. The buildings clung to a steep slope and were connected by a series of wooden stairs. River Camp had no shade, no showers or electric lights, and no system for cooling. Water was pumped from the river into huge metal tanks, and after sitting in the hot sun it was nearly undrinkable—a perfect breeding ground for bacteria, which led to an outbreak of dysentery among the men. Mice ran across the men's faces as they slept.

The average high temperature at River Camp was 119 degrees Fahrenheit, falling only to a low of 95 at night. Bob Parker, who worked in the mess hall (dining room) at River Camp, described the conditions in Andrew J. Dunar and Dennis McBride's book *Building Hoover Dam: An Oral History of the Great Depression*:

> It was a very well-laid-out kitchen, except it was very hot down there that summer. . . . In that kitchen, with all those big ranges and cookstoves, it was a fright in there. In those days we didn't have any air conditioning. One day [the boss] took about six or eight steps down through the kitchen in front of those big hot ranges, and he collapsed and died right there on the spot from heat prostration.
>
> We also had what we called the Ice Brigade. When somebody there in the canyon . . . became overcome with the heat, we dashed out there with these ice buckets and we'd pack them in ice. If their heart took it and they survived, OK. But if their heart stopped, that was it. We sent for the undertaker.

By the following summer, when Boulder City was built, conditions improved with the addition of air-conditioned dormitories and cold drinking water, but heat would continue to plague the dam workers in the canyon and the tunnels.

CALLING FOR A STRIKE

The terrible living and working conditions in Black Canyon, coupled with an announcement from Six Companies on August 7, 1931, of a wage cut for certain workers, led to a situation that was ripe for a strike. The labor union Industrial Workers of the World, called the IWW or the Wobblies, had been in the area for some time, hoping to enlist more men to join their union, which badly needed a boost in popularity and membership. The IWW's purpose was to protect workers' rights and their health and safety, and even among men who were grateful for any job at all, the conditions were nearly intolerable. After the announcement of wage cuts, the Wobblies held a meeting in the River Camp mess hall and the motion was made and voted on to go on strike. The strikers made a list of demands for Six Companies: issues such as canceling the pay cut and actually raising the minimum wage, rehiring the strike workers without discrimination, including the travel time from camp to site and back as part of the eight-hour shift, and providing ice water to the workers.

Unfortunately for the strikers, Six Companies rejected the demands and instructed all the strikers to pick up their paychecks and leave the project area. It was a harsh answer, but in a time of massive unemployment throughout the country, the company knew it could always find new workers to replace the strikers. Crowe summed up the company's refusal to negotiate to reporters: "We are six months ahead of schedule on the work now and we can afford to refuse concessions which would cost [us] $2000 daily."[8]

The perimeter of the work area was fenced in, and a new gate and guardhouse were constructed so that no one could enter the area without a government pass. Unfortunately, many men with families found themselves outside the gates while their families were still inside, camped in Ragtown. Merle Emery, who was the unofficial mayor of Ragtown and the owner of the town's only grocery store, said: "All working men were fenced out of the area. A big fence, with guards, about halfway between Boulder City and Railroad Pass. All of the workingmen were sent outside, and their families were left down at Ragtown. So I had all these women and kids—no men down there—to feed."[9] Eight days later the strike was over.

Despite the failure of the strike, it wasn't a total loss for the workers. Six Companies did install electric lights and water-coolers at River Camp and changing rooms with showers at the work site, and they accelerated the construction of Boulder City. Throughout all of this, however, work on the dam contin-ued at a relentless pace. There were many smaller projects to complete before the dam could actually be built.

THE DAM AND ITS COMPONENTS

The construction of the Hoover Dam was not just the construc-tion of the single, concrete wall to hold back the Colorado River. There were many smaller components of the project, any one of which would have been a major construction job in itself. The building of the dam would require not only new roads in and out of the canyon, but nearly twenty-one addi-tional miles of railroad track to connect the various areas of the site. Construction itself would require two concrete plants and a gravel-screening plant. Concrete, from which the dam would be made, was created by mixing sand and crushed rock, called aggregate, with Portland cement and water until it made a thick gray mud. Portland cement was a specific type of ce-ment, made of a heated mixture of finely ground limestone and clay, closely resembling a kind of stone quarried on the Isle of Portland off the British coast, from which it got its name. The aggregate had to be of a very high quality and a consistent size. The proper aggregate was found at a site six miles up-stream from the dam site.

A gravel-screening plant was built two miles west of the river. This plant was an enormous series of towers, tunnels, bunkers, and conveyor belts, all constructed in the desert out of more than 350 tons of structural steel, hauled there by rail-cars. The plant was built in a little over two months, at a cost of $450,000, and began operating in January 1932. There gravel was washed, sorted by size, and crushed so that it would be ready for mixing into concrete. Then the aggregate was loaded onto railcars and taken to one of the two concrete plants: the high-mix plant located on the Nevada rim of the canyon, and the low-mix plant, built on a shelf blasted into the cliffs three-quarters of a mile above the dam site. These two plants would provide all the necessary concrete to construct the various fea-tures of the dam.

AFTER THE STRIKE

In September 1931, after the strike initiated by the IWW failed, a dam worker named Claude Rader wrote a poem about how he and his fellow workers felt about their jobs at the Hoover Dam. In his book *Hoover Dam*, Joseph Stevens reprints a part of it:

Abe Lincoln freed the Negroes
And old Nero he burned Rome,
But the Big Six helped depression
When they gave the stiff a home.
In a nice bunk house they're sleepin'
They're workin' every day,
The hungry look has vanished
For they got three squares a day.
You'll find tall Lou from Kal-a-ma-zoo,
And Slim from Alabam,
Mixed in with all the rest of us
Old boys on Boulder Dam.

There are thousands we know that knock it
And holler that they are cheap,
But to us it brings no worry
Not a moments loss of sleep.
For we've been here since it started,
We're used to all the slam'
And we're stickin' to the finish
Us old boys on Boulder Dam.

The IWW responded with a parody of the poem called "Us Old Scabs on Boulder Dam." A scab was a term for someone who continued to work when others were on strike:

While they pay us coolies' wages
With a place to flop and eat.
So in the slaughterhouse inferno
You'll find us every day
Where the muddy Colorado
Rushes madly on its way.
And if the boys don't ORGANIZE
And quickly make us scram
We're sticking to the finish—
US OLD SCABS ON BOULDER DAM!"

Despite the IWW's continued efforts to organize at the dam project, they were never successful, and most likely that was due to the feelings of men like Claude Rader, who felt fortunate just to have a job with Six Companies.

BOULDER CITY RISES

Meanwhile, the construction of Boulder City and the proper housing of the dam workers and their families had begun. Homes were built in Boulder City according to the jobs of the men who would live in them. Men like Frank Crowe had beautiful Spanish-style homes complete with fireplaces and modern appliances. Senior engineers and administrators had slightly less grand homes, with the trend continuing down to the level of certain managers and engineers. The common workers would live in rows of one- , two- , or three-room cottages called dingbats. These little houses cost only a few hundred dollars to build, but they were rented to the workers for fifteen, nineteen, or

Housing developments like this one were built in Boulder City for workers on the Hoover Dam project. Although Boulder City was meant to be a temporary settlement, many workers stayed on after construction was completed.

AT HOME IN BOULDER CITY

By today's standards, a typical worker's house in Boulder City would be considered anything but luxurious. When the houses were being built, the construction workers were told to put speed ahead of craftsmanship. They were required to put up one and a half houses every day per each crew of two carpenters and a helper, and if they didn't meet the quota, they were fired. Because of this, the inside of each house was depressingly plain, with the barest minimum of necessities. The kitchen held a sink and a tiny gas range and oven, and the bathroom had a toilet and shower but no hot water. Naked light bulbs were used for lighting, the floor was plain wood, and the walls were thin with many cracks and loose joints. Outside, the yard consisted of nothing more than desert and sand, with very little that was green and growing.

But to families that had been living in tents, shacks, or cars, many of whom had lost their own homes because of the Depression, these tiny little houses were a luxury. They no longer had to cook over open fires or scoop water out of the river. Eventually these families would be able to afford furniture and appliances, and would have the time to decorate the inside of their homes as well as landscape their gardens.

Because so many houses were built so quickly, all the houses looked very similar. Sometimes an entire street would be built between the time a worker went to the dam and when he came home again eight hours later. Often men would end up in the wrong houses, as Rose Lawson, who once lived in Boulder City, describes in the book *Building Hoover Dam*: "Every house was exactly alike. You couldn't tell your own house. It was always a joke in the olden days about somebody coming into the wrong house. Men coming home from work—if they weren't thinking, they'd come into the wrong house. I do know of cases where people got up in the morning and found a man sleeping on their couch. But they'd just wake him and ask him what he was doing."

Boulder City was intended to be temporary, just there for the duration of the building of the Hoover Dam, but the workers and their families made the city home. At the end of the dam project, many families bought their homes from the government and stayed in Boulder City.

thirty dollars a month, depending on the number of rooms. The rent from these cottages would generate even more money for Six Companies over the course of the dam's construction.

Unmarried workers lived in big dormitories that were also built in Boulder City. For $1.64 a day, a man would get a small cubicle in the dormitory and three meals in the mess hall, as well as transportation to and from the work site in huge double-decker transport trucks called Big Berthas, which could carry 150 men. At the height of the dam's construction, 1,600 men would live in the dormitories of Boulder City.

Although intended to be only a temporary home for workers during the dam's construction, Boulder City soon took on a life of its own among those who lived there. It wasn't long before the streets of Boulder City, scraped from the desert by teams of mules pulling bladed wagons called Fresno scrapers (similar to a modern grader), were lined with all the elements of any American city. There were landscaped parks, stores, a movie theater, restaurants, churches, and eventually schools for all the workers' children. Those who lived in government houses tried to landscape their yards with cactus and other desert plants or, in an attempt by Boulder City to control the blowing sand, were given a reduction in their water bills if they tried to cultivate a lawn. Organizations and clubs formed, and those who had experienced the homelessness of the depression felt very fortunate to be forming a new community in the Nevada desert.

With Boulder City being constructed and workers living in better conditions, and as the preparation work of new roads, track, and gravel and cement plants were finished at the dam site, it was time to begin the first major project of the Hoover Dam: the construction of four huge diversion tunnels through the solid rock walls of Black Canyon.

THE FIRST BIG STEP **3**

Once the workers had been hired, the roads, railroads, and electricity put in place, and Boulder City construction under way, the first major aspect of the dam project could begin. On each riverbank, upstream of where the actual dam would be built, four large, white circles had been painted on the canyon walls. These circles, approximately fifty feet in diameter and twelve feet above river level, marked the locations for the four diversion tunnels that would be drilled through the solid rock of Black Canyon's walls. Excavating the diversion tunnels was an extremely critical step in constructing the dam, as they would allow the river water to bypass the dam site while it was being built.

DIVERTING THE RIVER

The diversion tunnels were vital to the Hoover Dam project. In order to build the actual dam, the river had to be rerouted around the site so that the riverbed could be pumped dry, excavated down to bedrock, and cleaned in order to make the best possible base for the enormous wall of concrete that would rise there. The diversion tunnels, two on each side of the river, would be fifty-six feet in diameter and cut through approximately four thousand feet of solid rock. These tunnels were as wide as a four-lane highway and as tall as a five-story building. Construction had to be completed by October 1, 1933, or else Six Companies would have to pay a fine of three thousand dollars a day to the government. If the tunnels were not completed in the prescribed timeframe, then there was no hope for completing the actual dam on time, so the government inserted the

Workers take a break in a diversion tunnel. The huge tunnels diverted the Colorado River to keep the riverbed dry for the construction of the Hoover Dam.

deadline into the contract as a way to ensure that the work would proceed according to schedule.

Adding to the pressure of this deadline was the fact that the tunnel could really only be excavated in the fall and winter. At other times of the year, the Colorado River was so swollen with water and silt from the mountain snowmelt that construction would be extremely difficult. The openings of the giant tunnels were also too big to drill and blast at one time, so they divided the openings into sections that would be excavated in a certain sequence. Each tunnel was circular in shape, and the first portion of the circle to be excavated was a twelve-foot-square shaft near the top that provided ventilation and access as the tunnels were enlarged. Then the wing sections, which were the two circular sides of the tunnel, were excavated. This left the huge bench sections, which were the thirty-by-fifty-foot rectangular centers of the tunnel, and once they were removed, the tunnel resembled a horseshoe forty-two feet high. The final step was to remove the curved, crescent-shaped floor of the tunnel, completing the full fifty-six-foot-diameter circle.

Once the tunnels were excavated, they would have to be lined with three feet of concrete before the water of the Colorado River could start flowing through them. This would prevent the rushing river water from eroding the rock walls of the tunnels.

DRILLING THE TUNNELS

Excavating the tunnel sections was a four-part process. First the facing, or rock surface, of the tunnel would be drilled with

THE MACHINE AGE

The Hoover Dam was one of the first major construction projects in America to rely almost completely on mechanized equipment. Horses and mules were involved very little in the process, except for the mules that pulled the large scrapers used to create the streets for Boulder City.

The Hoover Dam was built using large amounts of machinery: trucks, Caterpillar tractors, electric shovels, locomotives, a motorized cable system to carry concrete buckets, a gravel-screening plant with conveyor belts and automatic hoppers, and the power-driven drills used to carve the diversion tunnels. According to Joseph E. Stevens in his book *Hoover Dam*, "Frank Crowe had answered a reporter's question about the grand scale of operations in Black Canyon by remarking that 'this will be a job for machines.'"

The Hoover Dam also involved a huge amount of manpower. At the peak of construction, 5,218 men were employed on the project. The scope of the dam construction, especially in the midst of the Great Depression, was truly amazing to everyone who witnessed the activity in the Black Canyon. It was a new era of man-made structures and part of the new pace of America.

thirty holes, in five rows of six, deep enough to insert the dynamite for blasting. Once the drilling was completed, the powder men would insert the dynamite and the primers, which would fire the charge that ignited the explosive. Then the tunnel would be cleared of men and equipment and the switch would be flicked to set off the charge. After the blast, trucks and electric shovels would move in to scoop up the debris of rock (known to the workers as muck) and load it into trucks, on which it would be taken out of the canyon and dumped away from the site.

Drilling, blasting, and cleanup involved setting up scaffolding for the drillers to stand on and then removing it for every blast, which was extremely time-consuming on a job with such a tight deadline. Setting up and moving the scaffolding alone

Workers pose on their Williams Jumbo. This truck-mounted drill rig enabled workers to drill and blast tunnels more efficiently.

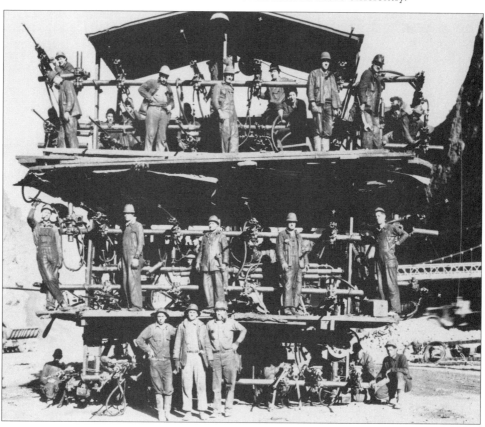

for years and as a result were crumbling, pitted with crevices and loose slabs of rock. To the men working in the canyon, even a small piece of rock falling a thousand feet could mean death if it hit them. Loose and unsteady rock would also jeopardize the structure of the dam if it crumbled where the concrete came into contact with the canyon walls, causing leaks or holes.

In order to prevent these safety and structural threats, the high scalers had the job of stripping the canyon walls of all loose rock and debris. The job was not for the nervous, because the high scalers did their work on ropes dangling hundreds of feet above the canyon. Small wooden platforms called bosun's chairs were rigged to these ropes, and the high scalers sat on them, rappelling up and down the canyon walls by loosening knots or climbing the ropes hand-over-hand. It took a specialized worker to make a good high scaler. In his book *Hoover Dam*, Joseph E. Stevens describes the high scalers:

HOMEMADE HARD HATS

Hard hats, which are now a familiar and required piece of equipment on every type of construction site, originally were not provided on the site of the Hoover Dam project. High scalers, clinging to the canyon walls by ropes, were in constant danger from falling objects, such as tools dropped by other workers or loose pieces of rock that were dislodged from the canyon itself.

Workers began to fashion protective headgear for themselves by dipping their standard cloth hats into hot tar and then letting them harden. Several layers of tar, cooled and redipped, would create a tough shell to protect the workers' heads. These homemade hard hats were extremely effective. Although workers were hit by falling objects severely enough to break their jaws, there were no reported skull fractures.

The contractors in charge of the dam project were impressed by these hats and ordered a supply of factory-made equivalents. Men in exposed areas were strongly urged to wear them. This made the Hoover Dam project the first hard-hat job in American history.

This monument depicts a high scaler clearing a canyon wall. High scalers performed dangerous work that required both strength and agility.

It was reported that many of the high scalers employed at Hoover Dam were former sailors or circus performers; sailor, acrobat or otherwise, they had to be agile and unafraid of dangling at the end of a slender line with nothing but air between them and the canyon floor far below. They also had to be strong, for they went over the side weighted down with wrenches, crowbars, water bags, and other paraphernalia.[12]

High scalers also had to find their way through a maze of ropes, electric lines, air hoses, dangling drill steel, and falling debris. Despite the constant danger of their position on the canyon wall, many high scalers could not resist performing stunts for the benefit of the workers below. They often competed to see who could push off and swing the farthest away from the wall, out over the canyon. It was even reported by other high scalers who witnessed the incident that one high scaler managed to swing out and catch the leg of an engineer who leaned out too far to inspect a portion of cliff and fell from the canyon rim. He held on to the man until a second high scaler swung over and pinned the man to the canyon wall and a line could be rigged to pull him to safety.

In the two years that the high scalers were at work on the canyon walls, they removed 137,000 cubic yards of rock. This amount of rock equaled a slab of rock one foot thick, ten city blocks long, and as high as New York City's Empire State Building.

With the high scalers cleaning up the canyon walls, and the diversion tunnels finished and lined with concrete, it was time to begin turning the river's flow into the tunnels so that the riverbed could also be prepared for the dam.

BUILDING A COFFERDAM

In order to force the Colorado River into the new diversion tunnels, cofferdams would have to be built just downstream from the four upper portals. The temporary dirt and rock dikes that had been built in front of the diversion tunnels to keep them dry during construction would be removed. Cofferdams were temporary dams, larger than the dikes, created by compacting loose rock and dirt to block the river from its usual bed and force it to flow into the tunnels.

On November 13, 1932, the dirt dikes in front of the tunnels were blasted away and water gradually entered the tunnels. A hundred dump trucks lined up on the road that led to the temporary vehicle bridge spanning the river just below the tunnel openings. Loaded with broken rock, they were ready to dump their loads into the muddy river water. The trucks began racing onto the bridge to dump the rock, racing back up to the rim for more muck, and racing down again. Every fifteen seconds a truck dumped a load of rock, ton after ton, until in the early hours of the following morning the river was finally blocked

A line of dump trucks wait to transport broken rock along the mountainside. Dumped into the river, the rock created cofferdams that rerouted the water into the diversion tunnels.

and pushed into the diversion tunnels. Two workers stood at the tunnel entrances with poles, pushing away bits of debris that might clog the openings. A crowd of spectators stood by to watch the river enter the tunnels and exit downriver. Al M. Rocca describes the scene in his book *America's Master Dam Builder: The Engineering Genius of Frank T. Crowe*:

> If the moment of inrushing water into the giant tunnel was not enough, eyewitnesses claimed that seeing, for the first time, thousands of gallons of raw, semi-tamed river water explode from the mouth of the exit portal, was a never to be forgotten memory. . . . First, nothing, then a rumble, then a small leakage of water and finally a shotgun-like explosion of dark white water, spraying outward and rushing onward as if suddenly released from captivity.[13]

The cofferdam was covered with a layer of concrete to keep the river water from eroding the dirt, and a second cofferdam was erected just upstream from the tunnel outlets, to keep river water from backing up into the work area.

The first and greatest step in the construction of Hoover Dam had been completed, a year ahead of schedule. With the river diverted, work could begin on preparing the riverbed for the massive concrete structure itself.

4

PREPARING THE
RIVERBED

By the spring of 1932, the diversion tunnels and cofferdams were done and the excess water had been pumped out of the riverbed between the temporary dams. Hundreds of pipe fitters, the men responsible for laying pipe systems, put in pipes, pumps, and air and water lines, and drained the last of the river water from the dam site. Everything was ready for the start of excavation for the foundations of Hoover Dam. Unfortunately, things were not going as smoothly in Washington, D.C.

MONEY TROUBLES

The Great Depression was deepening. That spring, American war veterans marched on Washington, D.C., demanding payment of their World War I bonuses. As the economy grew worse, Congress began to look for ways to eliminate all unnecessary funding. They took a hard look at the Hoover Dam project. To the eastern politicians, it was a project with no real benefits for their part of the country. With unemployment high and so many people in need, perhaps a huge dam project was a luxury. It was decided that the yearly project budget would be trimmed from ten million dollars to six million.

This caused panic with Six Companies and the Bureau of Reclamation. A budget cut would force them to delay or even shut down the project, as well as making it necessary to lay off workers. The two organizations lobbied Congress to restore their funding to the original level, arguing that in the long run, the budget cut would cost the government more money by extending the length of the contract past the original date of completion.

Unemployed Americans line up for food during the Great Depression. As the economy worsened, the budget for Boulder Dam was in danger of being cut.

Finally, President Hoover intervened. He pointed out that revenues to be collected from the finished dam would also be delayed. He asked that the money appropriated for the dam be increased, and finally a relief bill was passed to return funding to the Hoover Dam project. But Six Companies's problems with government policies had just begun.

A NEW SECRETARY

In 1933 Hoover lost the presidential election to Franklin Roosevelt. With a new administration there came a change in personnel that directly affected Hoover Dam. The new Secretary of the Interior Harold Ickes decided to closely examine the Hoover Dam project. His first act was to officially rename it Boulder Dam, rather than Hoover Dam, as it had been called from the start of construction. According to Ickes, "The name Boulder Dam is a fine, rugged, and individual name. The men who pioneered this project knew it by this name . . . These men, together with practically all who have had any first-hand knowledge of the circumstances surrounding the building of this dam, want it called Boulder Dam and have keenly resented the attempt to change its name."[14]

Secretary of the Interior Harold Ickes paid special attention to the Hoover Dam project.

Next he attacked the Six Companies policy of paying its workers in scrip. Scrip was basically credit that was redeemable at Six Companies–owned businesses such as the company store, although some businesses in Las Vegas would also accept it. Despite the argument that the use of scrip was standard practice with large companies, Ickes declared that the workingmen were entitled to receive their wages in tangible U.S. currency, and he ordered Six Companies to cease using scrip. The Boulder City manager was ordered to collect all the coupons and coins of scrip, redeem them for cash, and destroy them.

The third battle fought by Ickes and Six Companies was over the failure to hire black workers on the dam project. After the preliminary work on constructing roads and railroads, there had been almost no hiring of black workers, even those who were local to Las Vegas. Instead, most of the Hoover Dam workforce consisted of white workers from out of state. Even though the government's contract with Six Companies stipulated the hiring of any American citizen, this was mostly interpreted by Six Companies as meaning white American citizens.

When the dam's workforce reached a thousand without a single black man on the payroll, the Colored Citizens Labor and Protective Association of Las Vegas was formed to protest the discrimination. Six Companies argued that it had not hired blacks because it was afraid of creating conflict between the workers, and it had not wanted to have to build a segregated blacks-only dormitory. But in July 1932, the company gave in to the pressure and hired twenty-four blacks to work on the dam. This did not satisfy the Colored Citizens Association because this number still consisted of less than 1 percent of the entire dam workforce, and the black workers were employed in the gravel pits, one of the hottest and most remote areas of the dam project.

The National Association for the Advancement of Colored People (NAACP) complained to Secretary Ickes that not only were the numbers of blacks working on the dam extremely low, but they were also being excluded from living in Boulder City and were bused thirty miles from Las Vegas to the dam and back. Ickes investigated and found that the charges were true, and he was able to force Six Companies into at least letting the workers live in Boulder City, even though by the language of the government's contract he could do nothing to force increased hiring of minorities. The Hoover Dam workforce never even approached equality between white workers and black workers, but eventually those few black workers were integrated into Boulder City.

RACISM

In the America of the 1930s, racism was apparent everywhere and the Hoover Dam construction site was no different. Blacks worked laying track for the first railroad line to the dam area, but after that they were not included in the hiring for the project. However, Native Americans, including Yaqui, Crow, Navajo, and Apache, were employed as high scalers, swinging from cables and cleaning the canyon walls. They were allowed to live in the otherwise completely white environment of Boulder City.

After Secretary of the Interior Harold Ickes took office, he demanded that Six Companies hire more blacks. Six Companies responded by hiring a few more blacks, but they constituted less than 1 percent of the workforce and were employed in the gravel pits, or in other hot, monotonous jobs such as brushing the rust and scale from the steel that would be used in the dam. They were not allowed to live in Boulder City, but instead were bused along the bumpy Boulder Highway, thirty miles from the West Las Vegas slums to the dam site twice every day. At the work site they even had to drink from separate water buckets.

Six Companies argued that it did not want to have to build separate blacks-only dormitories in Boulder City and they were afraid of episodes of racial strife between the workers. Not all the residents of Boulder City seemed to feel that way, however. At one point, the Green Hut Café in Boulder City hired a black cook who was well known for baking wonderful pies. When the city manager told the owner of the café that he would have to fire the cook, the owner refused, claiming that the city manager could not tell him what to do unless he was prepared to buy his business first. As long as he owned the business, they could not tell him who to hire.

Eventually Ickes was able to decree that the few blacks on the project could live in Boulder City. Many of the white workers remember them for the wonderful rock work that they did on the parapets and walls along the highway near the dam and the spillways. There were not great numbers of blacks in the area until World War II, when a magnesium processing plant opened nearby and employed more minority workers.

MOVING AHEAD

Even as the political wrangling continued, the dam project moved ahead. In November 1932, the Colorado River Board, an independent body created by Congress to advise the Bureau of Reclamation on the engineering aspects of the dam, gave its final approval of the dam's design. Work could now proceed on preparing the riverbed for the actual dam construction.

The huge concrete mass of the dam would be locked into the canyon walls by huge, V-shaped cuts that would be carved into the rock walls. The high scalers were given this job, which required four months of time and 185 tons of dynamite. The cuts started at the top of the canyon walls and narrowed down four hundred feet to a point only a third of the way to the canyon floor. The dam would be "hooked" into these cuts, which would create additional strength where the concrete met canyon rock. From this point down there would be no more blasting in case it weakened the cliffs, whose strength was vital in holding back the huge mass of water that would collect in the reservoir lake. If the cliffs were damaged by blasting, severe leaks and dam failure where the concrete met the rock of the canyon walls could result.

IN THE RIVERBED

Down in the riverbed, the workers were busy removing the silt and gravel that had been building up for centuries. They used electric shovels, tractors, dump trucks, and often just huge numbers of men working by hand with shovels to clear the riverbed down to bedrock. The silt and gravel were then hauled out of the canyon and dumped into railroad cars, which transported them several miles upstream for disposal. It was an eerie place to work, accentuated by the stains of the river water on the cliffs, the sand and slimy gravel, stagnant pools of water, and a strong odor of decay. Frank Waters, a writer who visited Boulder Dam in 1933, describes the scene in the riverbed:

> One midnight . . . I stood on the bed of the river. The vast chasm seemed a slit through earth and time alike. The rank smell of Mesozoic ooze and primeval muck filled the air. Thousands of pale lights, like newly lit stars,

The diversion tunnels in the foreground drained the Colorado River. Workers then had to clean and dry the riverbed so construction could begin.

shone on the heights of the cliffs. Down below grunted and growled prehistoric monsters—great brute dinosaurs with massive bellies, with long necks like the brontosaurus, and with armored hides thick as those of the stegosaurus. They were steam shovels and cranes feeding on the muck, a ton at a gulp. In a steady file other monsters rumbled down, stopping just long enough to shift gears while their bodies were filled with a single avalanche, then racing backward without turning around. . . . All this incessant, monstrous activity took place in silence, in jungle heat, and as if in the . . . darkness of a world taking shape before the dawn of man.[15]

GETTING AROUND IN THE CANYON

The workers at the Hoover Dam had two ways of getting around the work site. These forms of transportation became famous, and were often pictured in newspaper stories and newsreel footage. The first was a device called a Joe McGee. The Joe McGee consisted of a small walled platform called a skip, attached to a cableway that could reel out the skip and drop it down into the canyon to a loading platform. A skip tender, a worker in charge of running the skip, would signal to the cable operator to move the skip and maneuver it up or down with its load of workers.

A worker on the dam, Harry Hall, describes the Joe McGee in the book *Building Hoover Dam: An Oral History of the Great Depression*: "They had what they called a Joe McGee, a high line that you could catch and go. They had landings on the water and also on the Arizona side. They had a cage that would transport maybe as many as twenty men perhaps. They would go into and across the canyon and also down at the same time. If you had any equipment or anything like that, you had to ride the Joe McGee."

It was not always an easy ride. The load cables would twist, causing the McGee to spin one way and then the other. Sometimes the signaling failed, and instead of stopping and dropping down to a loading platform, the Joe McGee would keep going straight into the canyon wall. One such accident in 1933 almost knocked the workers on board into the canyon below, and caused a number of hospitalizations for broken bones.

The other Hoover Dam transportation method was the monkey slide, a large platform that moved up and down on greased skids or rails. There were three monkey slides on the inclined face of the dam and another on the Nevada rim that went 850 feet below into the canyon and could carry fifty men. John Cahlan, another dam worker, describes the monkey slide in *Building Hoover Dam*: "They had what they called a monkey-slide, which was a sort of an open-air elevator. It went up the face of the dam when they built the thing. There were about 10 or 12 people that were on the monkey-slide, and it broke about halfway up the face of the dam and dumped them down onto a lot of steel piled on end. It just impaled three or four of these guys and bruised and injured the other people that were on the slide."

The workers continued to use dynamite and dig, trying to work down through the accumulated silt to find bedrock, the firm base of the river necessary to firmly anchor the massive concrete structure of the Hoover Dam. Twenty-two thousand cubic yards of material were hauled out of the canyon every day. The push for speed by superintendents and foremen led to a contest between diggers to see who could move the most muck on their shift. The winner was the swing shift crew on January 24, 1933, filling 1,841 truckloads, nearly four a minute, during their eight-hour shift.

FINDING THE RIVER BOTTOM

In his book *Hoover Dam*, Joseph Stevens describes the day when, after five months of digging, the shovels and diggers finally reached the bedrock below the riverbed:

> In mid-April, 1933, the steel jaws of the dragline buckets struck bedrock at [an] elevation . . . 40 feet beneath the river's level. From this elevation the bedrock shelved out from both canyon walls 150 feet to the middle of the canyon, then dropped sharply to form a V-shaped channel 75 feet deep. This narrow slot would make an excellent natural keyway for the dam's base, but first its filling of loose sand and gravel had to be dug out and its walls, which had been deeply carved and fluted by the whirlpools of the ancient river, had to be trimmed to create a uniform surface to which concrete could bond. [16]

Geologists determined that the deep ravine had probably been cut at the end of the last ice age. The bedrock had to be hosed cleaned, and scoured to be as clean, and dry as possible in order to bond with the concrete that would be poured on top of it. Pipes were laid in the slot to drain away any groundwater that seeped through the rock, and cracks were sealed with grout. Once the surface was prepared, the forms for the concrete could be built and the actual dam structure would begin to take shape.

BUILDING THE CABLEWAY

Before concrete could be poured on the dam structure, Six Companies needed to devise a method for transporting concrete from the two mixing plants to the work site as quickly as possible. In the less-than-perfect conditions in Black Canyon,

DYING ACROSS STATE LINES

There were many horrible accidents that took place at the Hoover Dam construction site, and many times there were bodies that had to be removed. By law, the body of an accident victim could not be moved until the county coroner had examined it at the scene of death. If the death took place on the Arizona side of the river, this meant that the coroner had to travel sixty-five miles through rough desert, which often took six hours. Many workers at the dam remember seeing bodies draped in bloody sheets, lying for hours at the base of the cliffs until the coroner arrived.

Workers quickly learned another difference between injury and death on the Arizona side of the river and the Nevada side. The state of Arizona paid more compensation money to accident victims or their survivors than the state of Nevada did. While the Colorado River was running at full flow, there was a three-hundred-foot expanse of water between the two states, but once the river was diverted and the riverbed was dry, the difference between states was no more than a thin line. If a man were killed in Nevada, other workers would surreptitiously drag his body into Arizona in order to better provide for his family. If a worker were injured in Nevada, he would often crawl onto the Arizona side, even with an injury like a badly broken leg, because he would be compensated at a higher rate.

Six Companies was very aware of this rate difference between states because it contributed to both states' insurance funds, and it tried to get the Arizona compensation rates reduced. They also tried to employ only single, unattached men whenever possible, minimizing the number of dependent families who might have to be paid in the event of a death. It had very little effect, however, and workers continued to claim to have their accidents in Arizona as often as possible.

concrete would harden before it could be poured on the dam structure if it could not be moved quickly enough.

The Bureau of Reclamation measured the uniformity and consistency of the concrete at the mixing plants. The concrete was tested by using the slump test, which involved filling a cone-shaped mold with concrete, removing the mold, and then measuring how much sag there was in the setting concrete. To meet the requirements of strength specified by the Bureau of Reclamation, the concrete had to be mixed very dry, with very little water. This resulted in concrete that was very difficult to work with, especially in the hot summer conditions, because the concrete would set or harden in the pouring buckets and then have to be returned to the plant to be chipped out by hand. In order to deliver the concrete quickly and efficiently and prevent it from hardening, Crowe used a cableway system, which he had first used in constructing Arrowrock Dam in Idaho in 1911. The cableway system would access all areas of the dam site, using buckets to pick up the concrete from rail cars and dump it at the required area. A government publication on the Hoover Dam describes the cableway:

> A group of heavy duty 25-ton capacity cableways were strung from rim to rim of the canyon at strategic points. These were five in number and were so located and devised that supplies could be deposited at any point on the dam, spillway open channels, intake towers, and most of the powerhouse. All of the cableway towers . . . were moveable . . . on parallel tracks and the end towers moved in unison, being operated by electric motors. The tendency of the tower to overturn was counteracted primarily by million-pound concrete blocks. All five cableways were operated from the head towers located on the Nevada side and were controlled by [telephone] orders from men in view of the loading and unloading activity.[17]

Each cableway had a wheeled carriage that ran along the cable track and could be moved back and forth across the canyon, a hoist cable that raised and lowered the load, and a dump line that released it. The main operator and the signalmen worked in perfect unison to control the loads. They picked up the loaded concrete buckets from the flatcars, swung them out over the canyon, lowered them to the place where they were needed, and then the operator hit the dump button to release the concrete.

The cableway system was vital to the construction of the dam, and fifty workers called riggers were responsible for regularly oiling and repairing the pulleys, track carriages, and

Workers prepare to pour the first load of concrete for the foundation of the Hoover Dam on June 6, 1933.

other parts of the system and constantly inspecting them for wear. Despite the endless inspections, sometimes the cables did fail without any warning and caused several deaths when workers were knocked off the dam by careening buckets, which would then smash into the canyon walls and shatter like bombs. Even with the accidents, however, some workers would actually "ride the hook," hitching a ride on a bucket for a quick trip to the canyon rim.

READY TO POUR

The cable system was completed, the two concrete-mixing plants were ready for production, and the riverbed had been dredged, cleaned, and scoured. Everything was finally ready for the pouring of Hoover Dam. The first wooden forms for the concrete that would shape the dam had been constructed, resembling a series of square wooden rooms without roofs or floors. On June 6, 1933, at 11:20 A.M., the first bucket of concrete swung off its flatcar, up and over the canyon, and was released into the first form. Hoover Dam had finally begun to take shape.

BUILDING THE DAM

The two years of site preparation were finished and it was finally time for the construction of the actual dam. This would require a high degree of cooperation between thousands of men, millions of cubic yards of concrete, and Frank Crowe's complicated cable system for delivering materials quickly to where they were needed. The concrete dam would have to be poured and cooled as quickly as possible without compromising the quality and integrity of the finished mass of concrete that would be responsible for holding back the Colorado River.

USING CONCRETE

To understand the methods used for pouring the concrete for the Hoover Dam, it is necessary to understand exactly what concrete is made of and how it cures and hardens. Concrete is made from crushed stone, sand, and cement, and when water is added the cement goes through a chemical process called hydration. Through this process, crystals are formed that tie themselves and the rest of the ingredients together. The process creates the strength of the concrete, but it also produces considerable heat. If cooling takes place too quickly or too unevenly, cracks can form in the concrete, and this has to be avoided in dam construction because cracks would weaken or even destroy the dam structure.

If the Hoover Dam had been constructed by pouring one solid wedge of concrete the size of the finished dam, it would have taken at least one hundred and fifty years to cool completely, and the risks of cracks from uneven cooling would have made the structure unstable. This meant that the Hoover Dam would have to be constructed as a series of smaller concrete forms that would be

This concrete mixing plant contributed to the millions of cubic yards of concrete needed to build the Hoover Dam.

cooled with ice water running through pipes imbedded in the concrete. Later these same pipes would be filled with grout, a thin concrete mixture that could be pumped through the water pipes and would harden to make the dam one solid mass. An eight-foot wide slot was left in the center of the dam structure to hold the large pipes that carried the cold water between the dam and a refrigeration plant where the cooling water was chilled. This slot would later be filled in as the dam grew higher and neared completion.

CONSTRUCTING THE CONCRETE FORMS

To create the dam structure, concrete would be poured into wooden forms. The plan was to construct the dam as a series of 230 vertical columns, with their sides keyed to each other by horizontal or vertical grooves that would interlock. Each column

STATE CONTRIBUTIONS

During the construction of the Hoover Dam, nearly every state in the Union contributed some sort of building material or expertise to its construction. The biggest contribution was the workforce. Men came from all over the United States during the 1930s to work on the dam. The average man was thirty-five years old. Forty percent were unmarried. On most work days there were three thousand men in the workforce.

Forty-seven states contributed other materials to the dam project. These contributions ranged from chickens for the mess hall in Boulder City (from Arkansas), to three of the original Six Companies (from California), to crescent wrenches for all the dam workers (from Connecticut), to granite for the terrazzo floors in the powerhouse (from New Hampshire). Ohio and Pennsylvania manufactured the steel, the turbines for the power plant came from Virginia and Wisconsin, and a company in Delaware provided aerial photography of topography and ground surveys. The concrete research used to build the dam was a joint participation of three universities, the U.S. Bureau of Standards, and the Portland Cement Association of Chicago. Just about every state in the United States can claim that it contributed to some aspect of the Hoover Dam, which is part of what makes the dam a national monument as well as a utilitarian structure.

In addition to American companies and suppliers, several foreign countries also had a part in the Hoover Dam. Italian craftsmen worked on the terrazzo floors. Generators and other electrical equipment came from Canada, Japan, Sweden, and Holland. A German company produced the overhead cranes in the power plant, and the bronze sculptures and star chart were designed by Oskar Hansen, a Norwegian immigrant.

was approximately twenty-five feet by sixty feet, built up five feet at a time. The forms that held the wet concrete were staggered instead of being constructed side by side in rows, so that they could be maneuvered more easily. This gave each block the maximum amount of exposure to the air for cooling before another block was poured beside it. As the dam was built, these forms looked like tall skyscrapers without windows, or as Joseph Stevens describes them in his book *Hoover Dam*, "a jumble of concrete boxes rising upwards in fits and starts, a horizontal five-foot-thick layer poured first on one column, then on another."[18]

Small tunnels and rooms, used as access for grouting, drainage, and inspection, were also built into the structure, as well as elevator shafts for accessing the lower rooms and the powerhouse.

THE COOLING SYSTEM

In order to cool all the concrete as it was poured, a system had to be built to supply an endless amount of cooled river water to the dam. The temperature of the water also had to be adjustable depending on the air temperature and conditions within the dam's concrete.

A total of 662 miles of cooling pipe was embedded in the dam in each poured block, one of the biggest networks of interconnected tubing that had ever been attempted in a building project. Each five-foot-thick block of concrete was honeycombed with one-inch-diameter tubing, which connected with bigger water pipes running through an open slot down the center of the dam. The tubing and pipes were connected to a refrigeration plant built a few hundred yards downstream on the Nevada side of the river, where a compressed ammonia system cooled the water to forty degrees Fahrenheit and then sent it through the tubing within the dam. Thermometers were also imbedded in the concrete so that the dam's internal temperature could be constantly monitored and the water temperature adjusted accordingly. When the concrete's temperature hit normal in a particular layer of the dam, the water could then be shut off to those tubing loops with preinstalled valves. Eventually the tubes and pipes would be filled with grout to make the dam a solid mass. A government publication on the Hoover Dam describes the cooling process:

Giant concrete blocks dry in wooden forms in the riverbed. These blocks provided the foundation of the Hoover Dam.

Cooling of water was accomplished by . . . an ammonia refrigeration plant, which if turned to ice production could have produced 1,000 tons in 24 hours. Fourteen-inch pipes carried the cooling water to a slot of eight-foot width in the center of the dam, where connections were made to the smaller cooling headers and tubing. Water flowed through the cooling loops at the rate of four gallons per minute. The [entire] structure was cooled in a period of 20 months and grouting finished shortly thereafter.[19]

A CONCRETE ASSEMBLY LINE

The next challenge to pouring the dam was in the transportation and delivery of the huge buckets of concrete. The low-mix concrete plant, already in use for other parts of the dam, was put into full production. Trains consisting of one engine and one flatcar moved between the dam and the concrete plant. Railroad flatcars were modified, with four compartments that were walled on the back side but open on the canyon side, so that a fresh bucket of concrete could be placed in each compartment and could be easily accessed on the open side by the hooks on the cable system. Workers could stand on the railcar's partition walls, enabling them to hook and unhook buckets quickly. The train would move into place and stop beneath the waiting cable connector. The workers hooked the concrete buckets onto the cable and they were hoisted away to be poured onto the dam. The entire system was designed to bring concrete from the low-mix plant as quickly as possible, hook the buckets to the cable system, and deliver them to the forms on the growing dam. This procedure was repeated constantly, twenty-four hours a day. Curley Francis, who ran one of the locomotives, describes his part of the job:

> You had to be quite efficient with air brakes when hauling concrete to the cableways, due to the fact that you had to stop right on the money in order to receive the empties and move the length of the bucket for the cableway to pick up the full load. . . . These concrete buckets . . . when they were full of eight yards of [concrete], they weighed 24 tons. You picked up your concrete . . . and you went about 60 feet to the cable. Everybody hated it because it was back and forth, back and forth, back and forth all the time.[20]

FILLING THE FORMS

Once the buckets of concrete were delivered to the wooden forms on the dam, the workers would open the safety catches on the bottom of the buckets and the concrete would be dumped into the form. The concrete surface underfoot had been cleaned off with jets of water, the cooling tubing had been laid out, and the area covered with a layer of grout before the concrete was poured. Workers called puddlers would

TWO DEATHS

One of the first fatalities to take place at the Hoover Dam site occurred on December 20, 1922, when J.G. Tierney, part of the Bureau of Reclamation drilling team exploring Black and Boulder Canyons, was swept off a barge and drowned in the Colorado River. By an uncanny coincidence, the very last fatality on Hoover Dam also took place on December 20, 1935, exactly thirteen years later. To make it even more unusual, the worker killed was Patrick Tierney, J.G. Tierney's son. He was a twenty-five-year-old electrician's helper working on the top of one of the intake towers when he slipped and fell 350 feet to his death.

stand in the wet concrete and push it around with their feet, to make sure that there were no air pockets and that the concrete mixture had not separated while in the bucket. The puddlers would stomp up and down, or use a tool called an agitator, which vibrated the concrete like a mixer.

One bucket would raise the level of concrete in the form by about two feet. Although there is a persistent mythology that says workers were buried in the concrete, this small amount of concrete wouldn't even cover a man's body if he happened to fall in it. Despite this fact, it is still the most enduring myth about the Hoover Dam, perhaps because it makes the huge, impersonal dam seem more personal if people envision it as a tomb for unfortunate workers. The only man who ever came close to being buried in the dam structure was W.A. Jameson, a worker killed when a panel of one of the wooden forms collapsed, plunging him to the bottom of the dam and covering him with a load of concrete. His body was recovered from the concrete after sixteen hours of digging.

Although each form could be filled with several buckets of concrete, the amount of cement needed to produce the concrete necessary for building the Hoover Dam equaled the entire production of four cement plants in the western United States. Because the cement coming from all these different plants would vary in color, the high-mix cement plant actually had a blending silo where the different colors were mixed together. This resulted in a completed dam that was all one

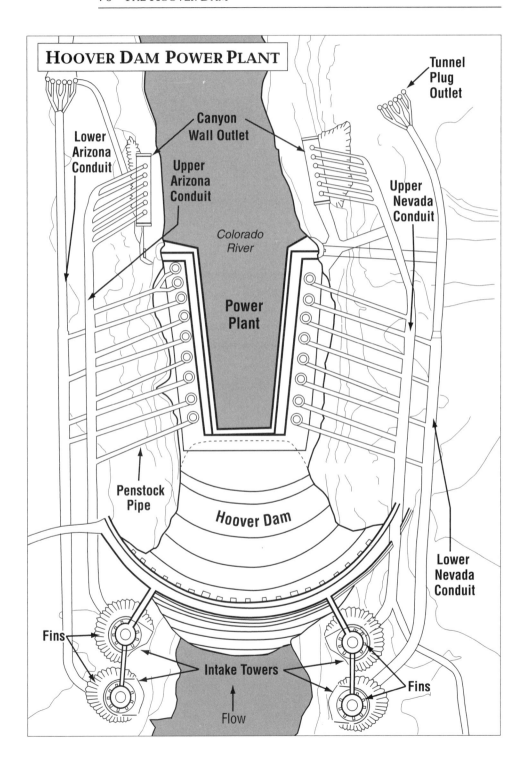

HOOVER DAM POWER PLANT

Tunnel Plug Outlet

Canyon Wall Outlet

Lower Arizona Conduit

Upper Arizona Conduit

Upper Nevada Conduit

Colorado River

Power Plant

Penstock Pipe

Lower Nevada Conduit

Hoover Dam

Fins

Intake Towers

Fins

Flow

color, instead of a checkerboard pattern of the blocks created from different-colored cements. This attention to detail helped make the Hoover Dam a beautiful structure as well as a utilitarian one.

As the dam structure was rising, other components of the dam were also being built as Six Companies tried to get everything done at the same time. Because of all this activity, employment at the dam reached its peak of 5,251 men in July 1934. As Crowe described the situation, "We had 5,000 men in a 4,000 foot canyon. The problem . . . was to set up the right sequence of jobs so [the workers] wouldn't kill each other off."[21] This was especially important as work began on the intake towers and other structures necessary to water control on the dam.

TOWERS, SPILLWAYS, AND GLORY HOLES

The intake towers, through which the water in the reservoir would flow into the power plant in controlled amounts, were being built on shelves hacked out of the canyon walls above the dam. Looking at the dam today, the towers seem to rise out of the middle of the lake, but they were actually built on the river banks 250 feet above the old riverbed, which allowed river silt to collect on the river bottom while water flowed in through the towers at a higher level. This reduced the amount of silt flowing through the pipes of the dam. This method helped the future reservoir behind the dam perform its important function of collecting silt. Each 395-foot-high tower was a hollow concrete cylinder with twelve fins projecting from the center like spokes on a wagon wheel. Steel trash racks (grates that kept debris from entering the gate openings) spanned the openings between the fins. Each tower had two gates, one at the bottom and one 150 feet higher, which weighed approximately half a million pounds each and were opened and closed by a hoist on top of the tower. Just as in the dam, forms were used to construct the towers, each form raising the tower by ten feet. Reinforcement steel was placed in the concrete to strengthen the tower structures. Each bucket of concrete would add two feet at a time to the form. It would take roughly sixteen work hours to pour a complete two-foot layer around the entire circle of one tower.

Spillways were constructed upstream from the dam and at a height nearly the same as the finished dam. These would serve to handle any overflow from high water or flooding that would threaten to spill over the top of the dam, weakening it. The spillways were 650 feet long and 170 feet deep, excavated out of the canyon walls behind the dam abutments on both sides. These spillways were so large that if they were dammed, a large battleship could float in them. The spillways had steel drum gates that could be opened to allow water to run into them and down steep tunnels that joined the diversion tunnels and emptied into the river below the dam.

These steep tunnels at the end of the spillways were called glory holes. They were seventy feet wide and swooped downward at a forty-five-degree angle until they met the lower portion of the outer diversion tunnels. Excavating these tunnels and lining them with concrete was extremely difficult because

Intake towers in the reservoir (pictured) allow water to flow into the Hoover Dam power plant, which generates hydroelectric power.

HOW A GENERATOR WORKS

The Hoover Dam power plant has a total of seventeen generators to convert the energy of the Colorado River water into hydroelectric power. The process that creates this power begins with the water that enters the intake towers in the reservoir. As it enters the towers, it falls through the tunnels inside the canyon walls and into the steel penstock pipes. The water rushing through the pipes spins a turbine (a bladed wheel), which then turns a shaft or axle connected to a rotor, which is a second wheel lined with magnets. An exciter sends an electric current to this rotor, charging it with a magnetic field. As the water spins the turbine, the shaft, and the rotor, the rotor spins inside the stator, a tightly wound coil of wire. This creates a moving magnetic field that causes an electric current to move through the stator. This current, at 16,500 volts, leaves the generator and is carried to the transformers, where it is increased to up to 230,000 volts before it leaves the dam and is transmitted through huge power lines across the countryside.

One of the curiosities of the Hoover Dam power plant is the "gold room," the name given to the room containing the heavy copper bars that carry electricity from the generators to the transformers. The cabinets surrounding these bars are also solid copper, and the name probably comes from the bright gold finish on these cabinets. Rumors have persisted, however, that the metal has a high gold content.

the tunnels grew smaller in diameter as they sloped into the canyon walls. This made it difficult to construct forms for pouring the concrete. The slope also made it hard to transport materials. The workers attempted to pour the concrete using a pipeline, but they were not able to keep the inside of the pipe cool and wet, and the extreme temperatures within the tunnels made the concrete harden as soon as it entered the hot metal pipe. Finally Crowe's talent for creating new equipment led to the use of a portable agitator, which would mix the concrete and keep it workable as a cable car transported it down into the tunnel. There was a spectacular accident, though, when a concrete-pouring form broke loose within the tunnel and slid down the entire length of the tunnel with three men aboard, moving faster and faster until it came out of the diversion tunnel into the river below. Amazingly, all three men survived the three-quarter-of-a-mile ride through the glory hole and the Arizona cliffs.

The other aspect of constructing the dam dealt with the piping that would deliver water to the powerhouse. These penstock pipes, as they were called, were so difficult to produce that they required a separate government contract just to cover the cost of their construction.

FABRICATING THE PENSTOCK PIPES

In order to supply the dam's power plant with the water it needed to generate electricity, narrow penstock tunnels had to be drilled into the cliffs on both sides of the river. Water entered the intake towers into huge, thirty-foot-diameter penstock header pipes from which eight penstock pipes branched off and angled into the powerhouses. Excess water could be shunted past the powerhouses into the old diversion tunnels and discharged back into the river from valve houses on the canyon walls.

Unlike the other tunnels of the Hoover Dam, which were lined with concrete, the penstocks would be lined with fitted steel pipes that had to be fabricated and installed. The steel lining was necessary because of the volume of water that would be passing through the pipes at all times. Constructing this pipe was such a specialized job that it required a separate contract, which was awarded to the Babcock & Wilcox Company of Ohio.

Because of the piping's large size, some of it thirty feet in diameter, there was no way to transport it from a factory to the dam site, as there was not a truck or railroad flatcar big enough to carry it. To solve this problem, Babcock & Wilcox built a complete steel fabrication plant at the site, with all the necessary machinery: a furnace, a bending mill, a vertical rolling mill, and X-ray machinery for checking metal welds. This factory cost nearly $600,000 and employed more than one hundred people. In the spring of 1933, production began that would transform forty-four thousand tons of steel into piping for the dam. The steel would be rolled into huge pipes and the sections welded and then X-rayed to make sure that the welds were good. Then

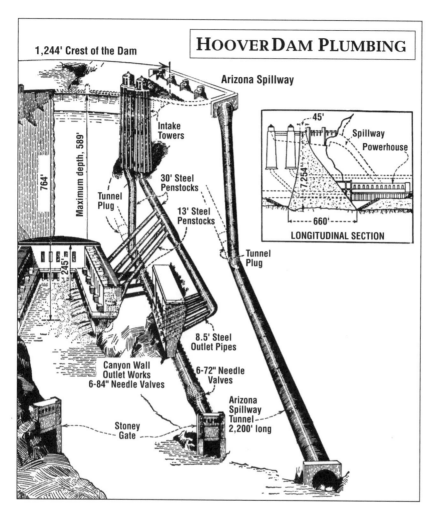

HOOVER DAM PLUMBING

1,244' Crest of the Dam

Arizona Spillway

Intake Towers

Maximum depth, 589'

764'

Tunnel Plug

30' Steel Penstocks

13' Steel Penstocks

245'

Tunnel Plug

8.5' Steel Outlet Pipes

Canyon Wall Outlet Works 6-84" Needle Valves

6-72" Needle Valves

Arizona Spillway Tunnel 2,200' long

Stoney Gate

45'

Spillway Powerhouse

7,254'

660'

LONGITUDINAL SECTION

the pipe would be "baked" in a big oven, heated to 1,150 degrees Fahrenheit and then cooled gradually so that it would withstand the expansion and contraction that would take place as water flowed through the pipes.

The huge sections of pipe were then transported to the dam on specially designed truck trailers. After they arrived, they were picked up by a huge government-owned cable system that would be a permanent part of the dam complex, swung over the canyon rim, and brought down into the canyon. Each pipe had a "spider" inside it, which was a brace of metal segments that stiffened the pipe and kept it from becoming egg-shaped when picked up by the crane.

LAS VEGAS

As the Hoover Dam construction project drew to a close, it was expected that Las Vegas would slip back into its former existence as a sleepy country town. Las Vegas, though, seemed to have other plans, mostly due to three important circumstances.

In 1931, gambling was legalized in the state of Nevada. This led to the opening of clubs and casinos that catered to the dam workers, but were later found to be just as much of a draw for out-of-town visitors as the Hoover Dam. In 1933, Roosevelt's administration launched the New Deal, which provided money for jobs and projects all over the country to benefit those put out of work by the Great Depression. Because of New Deal projects, Las Vegas received newly paved streets, new sewer lines, landscaped public parks, and new public buildings, making the city more attractive to visitors and new businesses alike. Finally, the unexpected popularity of Hoover Dam as a tourist destination also worked in Las Vegas's favor. In 1934 and 1935, three-quarters of a million tourists visited the dam and were also drawn to Las Vegas for hotels, restaurants, and gambling.

In the early 1940s, the U.S. Army Air Force opened a training school and gunnery range near Las Vegas, and Basic Magnesium built a magnesium plant nearby. World War II swelled the numbers of defense workers and military personnel in the area.

Lake Mead's popularity as a recreational area for boating, fishing, and exploring also drew people to the Las Vegas area, as a new water vacation spot in the desert. Tourism to the lake and the dam continues to be strong, requiring more businesses in the food and lodging industry.

It would take a year to install and weld together the entire network of penstock pipes. They had to be maneuvered into place through what are now observation tunnels, fitted together, and then riveted. Often the pieces would not quite fit and workers would have to apply dry ice or heat to sections of pipe to make it expand or contract.

Once the penstocks were in place and functioning, and the diversion tunnels were no longer handling all of the river's flow, the old diversion tunnels were plugged above the point where the penstock pipes intersected them. This was to prevent water from backing up during flooding. It was at this time that the end was in sight for the construction of Hoover Dam.

FINISHING UP

In December 1934, the 3-millionth cubic yard of concrete was poured on the Hoover Dam. Sixty-three days later, the first column of the dam structure was topped off at 726 feet, the final height of the dam. Once the entire dam reached this height, workers began to put cofferdams in front of three of the diversion

This aerial photo shows the Hoover Dam and its reservoir, Lake Mead. Lake Mead is the nation's largest man-made reservoir.

tunnels, forcing the Colorado River to flow through just one tunnel. Finally a concrete plug was poured for the fourth diversion tunnel. This plug contained four six-foot-diameter holes, which were fitted with valves that could be opened or closed. Enough river water could pass through these valves to meet the irrigation needs of California's Imperial Valley, while the rest would begin pooling behind the dam and creating Lake Mead, the Hoover Dam's reservoir. On February 1, 1935, a steel bulkhead gate weighing more than one thousand tons closed off the portal of the last open tunnel. The river was forced through the tunnel with the plug and would now be totally controlled by man.

This day also marked the beginning of the end of the dam's construction as the workforce dropped below four thousand and the rest of the workers began to look for new jobs elsewhere.

Muddy water slowly began to pool behind the dam and form the basis for the new reservoir. Leo Dunbar, a Hoover Dam worker, describes the effects on the dam as water began rising behind it:

> There was quite a bit of water coming in around the dam area. After February 1935, when they closed the gates and started raising the reservoir, we began to have trickles down the canyon, everywhere below the dam. [Water] was going around what grouting they had done as they poured the dam. The only explanation for that was that as the water raised in the reservoir, it was finding voids [in the rock]. As the water raised, it would get into one of those [voids] and the sides of [the canyon] would begin to slide in or tumble in. The same thing was happening in the river here, [as] great walls of sandstone, loose stuff . . . would fall into the river.[22]

Another worker, Harry Hall, describes the earthquake tremors that occurred as the reservoir filled: "The filling of the lake and the tremendous amount of weight from the water caused the crust of the earth to change position. We had a tremendous number of earthquakes—not fatal ones, but you could see the dust fly, you could hear, you could feel some of them."[23] As the reservoir filled over the years, however, these tremors gradually ceased.

There was not much left to do. The powerhouse was completed, a U-shaped building that ran along the canyon walls and the base of the dam. It was as long as six city blocks and was twenty stories high, although half of that height would be hidden by the low water on the backside of the dam. Made of concrete and structural steel to withstand any rock falls from the canyon walls, the powerhouse contained seventeen generator units and could produce enough energy to serve 1.3 million people a year. For ten years, from 1939 to 1949, Hoover Dam would be the world's largest hydroelectric installation.

Most of the work left to do on the dam was either cosmetic or cleanup, such as grinding and patching concrete, tiling the floors of the galleries that ran through the dam structure, tearing down temporary buildings, dismantling machinery, and preparing equipment to be shipped to the sites of new dam construction projects. Men received their layoff slips and headed off to work on other jobs, and Boulder City slowly emptied. The Hoover Dam project was drawing to a close.

6

THE FINAL TOUCHES

The Hoover Dam was nearly completed by late summer 1935. It had been finished in less than five years, two years ahead of schedule according to the original government contract. All that remained to finish the dam were the final decorative touches, which are still an important aspect of visiting the dam today. Hoover Dam is not only a functioning method of water control, but also a national landmark and a symbol of the American West. With that status in mind, every effort was made to create a structure that was as attractive as it was functional.

DECORATING THE DAM

Hoover Dam, as well as being an important method for controlling the Colorado River, is also a breathtaking sight. Much of this is due to the architects and artists who contributed to the finished details of the structure. The first of these men was an architect named Gordon B. Kaufmann, who was responsible for making the dam something more than the utilitarian mass of concrete designed by the engineers.

Kaufmann, a native of London, England, had been brought to Boulder City to help design the administration building there. He was asked to comment on the design of the dam as well, and he ended up redesigning it to make the dam attractive as well as useful. He replaced details of the original plan, such as a strange motif carved into the top of the dam and a pair of massive eagle statues perched on top of the access towers. He changed the look of the four protruding access towers (containing elevators and stairways into the interior of the dam) originally located on the face of the dam, blending them into the

Water gushing over the Hoover Dam's Arizona Spillway is a magnificent sight. Architect Gordon B. Kaufmann enhanced the dam to make it aesthetically pleasing.

surface, and he also smoothed the top portions of the four intake towers. The result was a dam that looked smooth and modern. Although these design changes took place in the earliest planning of the dam, it was not until the project was completed that the effect of his total design became most apparent.

Another person responsible for the final Hoover Dam decoration was Allen True, a Denver, Colorado, artist who assisted Kaufmann with interior designs and colors. The official Hoover Dam website describes True's designs for the terrazzo floors inside the dam structure:

> True was responsible for one of the dam's most distinctive motifs—the Southwestern Indian designs in the terrazzo floors. Using such sources as an Acoma bowl and

Pima basket, True linked Native American geometric concepts with Art Deco design. Many of the Indian designs were based on centrifugal themes, which related to the turbines of the power plant. True's colors were truly striking. He used black, white, green, and dull-red ochre chips in the terrazzo floor to contrast with the black-marble walls. True also specified the red color for the generator shells in the power plant, a sight that still commands visitors' attention.[24]

The terrazzo floors were actually installed by two Italian immigrant brothers, Joseph and John Martina, who worked for the J.B. Martina Mosaic Company of Denver, Colorado. To create the floors, the workers embedded marble chips in cement, separating them with strips of brass or aluminum to make the tiled patterns.

THE PHOTOGRAPHS OF BEN GLAHA

The best records of the construction of Hoover Dam, and some of our most familiar images of it, are the photographs taken by Ben Glaha, a senior engineer draftsman in the Bureau of Reclamation. In 1931, the bureau decided that the Hoover Dam project needed photographic documentation, and Ben Glaha was hired to chronicle the process.

Glaha essentially produced publicity for the bureau, so he avoided taking pictures of strikes, injuries, and deaths. His job was to convince the public of the importance of the dam project and how it would improve their quality of life, and to stress productivity, safety, and thrift. Glaha had an artist's eye, however, and many of his photographs of the dam go far beyond just a record of construction. His photographs inspired other photographers such as Ansel Adams, who also photographed Hoover Dam. In 1934 Glaha produced a portfolio of forty-four photographs of the dam, which were distributed to government officials as a souvenir of the dam. He also went on to exhibit his photos in many museums, beginning in January 1935. They later went on to tour the country. Today his photos are still owned by the Bureau of Reclamation, but some are in the collection of the Library of Congress.

After the mosaic hardened, huge finishing machines were used to polish the surfaces until they were glossy and shining.

On the Nevada side of the dam stands a dedication monument, consisting of two huge winged figures and a flagpole, surrounded by a star map inset into the floor. The terrazzo star map was designed by Oskar J.W. Hansen, a Norwegian-born artist who, following a national competition for this honor, was appointed as a consulting sculptor to the project by Secretary of the Interior Ickes. This star chart or celestial map preserves for the future the exact placement of the stars and planets on September 30, 1935, the day of President Roosevelt's dedication of the Boulder Dam. This map is so precise that future generations, if they did not already know the date of dedication, could calculate it exactly from the star chart alone. The map also includes a compass and the signs of the zodiac.

Harry Hall, a dam worker, describes the creation of the star map:

> Leland Robinson ran the instruments for [Hansen] to locate the stars and the constellations on the star map. He had drawings that showed the declination and angle between each one. Leland would turn the angles where he'd measure the distance. They would be set, and then the terrazzo was placed to conform with the star map. However, in years later the temperature and the terrazzo didn't get along too well. So the terrazzo began to crack and had to be removed. Oskar J. Hansen was right back on the job. He didn't want anyone else fooling around with his star map. So they put another surface around there. There was a different mix. So far it's worked out OK.[25]

Hansen also sculpted the winged sculptures of the dedication monument. He called them the Winged Figures of the Republic. Thirty feet high, they were cast out of more than four tons of statuary bronze, and they rest on a base of black diorite, a highly polished black stone. In order to place the statues on the blocks without scratching the polished finish, they were centered on blocks of ice and maneuvered precisely into place as the ice melted.

Hansen described his statues as representing mankind itself, and he compared the Hoover Dam to other famous works such as the Great Pyramids of Egypt: "The building of Hoover

One of Oskar J.W. Hansen's Winged Figures of the Republic is pictured here. Hansen designed the sculptures to commemorate the completion of the Hoover Dam.

Dam belongs to the sagas of the daring. The winged bronzes which guard the flag therefore wear the look of eagles. To them also was given the vital upward thrust of an aspirational gesture; to symbolize the readiness for defense of our institutions and keeping of our spiritual eagles ever ready to be on the wing."[26]

Finally, Hansen designed a plaque commemorating the ninety-six men who died during the construction of the dam, as well as other bas-relief designs on the elevator towers. The plaque, which was originally set into the canyon wall but was moved to a spot near the winged sculptures, reads: "They died to make the desert bloom. The United States of America will continue to remember that many who toiled here found their final rest while engaged in the building of this dam. The United States of America will con-tinue to remember the services of all who labored to clothe with substance the plans of those who first visioned the building of this dam."[27]

With the final touches completed on the dam, the day came for the official dedication of Hoover Dam.

DEDICATION DAY

The traffic on the highway between Las Vegas and the Hoover Dam was bumper to bumper on the morning of September 30, 1935, as many people headed for the dedication ceremonies. Dressed in their Sunday best, spectators packed the dam area, and by the end of the day at least twelve-thousand people had visited the dam. At 9:30 A.M., a train carrying the president of the United States, Franklin D. Roosevelt, pulled into Union Pacific Station in Las Vegas. An open touring car carried the president and his entourage to the dam. As he was seated in a

LOSING THE PRESIDENT

During President Roosevelt's visit to the Hoover Dam for the dedication ceremonies, an incident occurred during which he was actually lost to the Secret Service for several hours. He had been persuaded to visit another canyon nearby where other government-funded work had been done. Roosevelt left without the knowledge of his security people or Mrs. Roosevelt. Essentially this meant that for two hours the United States did not have a president because he could not be reached. His car had gotten stuck at the end of a dead-end road. After an hour and a half without any contact with the president, the security force began heading for the canyon but met the president's car coming back. The Secret Service felt relief only when President Roosevelt finally returned to Las Vegas and was safely aboard his train. Afterward, many officials wondered how it would have been explained if the president's car had been found wrecked at the bottom of a canyon, where he had never been cleared by security to go in the first place.

President Franklin D. Roosevelt tours the Hoover Dam before the official dedication ceremonies.

special speaker's platform erected on the Nevada side, the president's first comment was, "Gee, this is magnificent!"[28]

The president made his official address from his vantage point in a specially erected roofed platform above the dam and the slowly rising Lake Mead. "This is an engineering victory of the first order—another great achievement of American resourcefulness, skill, and determination. That is why I have the right once more to congratulate you who have created Boulder Dam and on behalf of the nation to say to you, Well done."[29]

HANDING OVER THE DAM

Despite the congratulations and the official dedication ceremony, the dam was not actually completed until the Department of the Interior agreed that Six Companies had fulfilled the contract and released it from further obligation. The government continued to request that Six Companies install additional power equipment, transmission lines, roads, and other extras before it would declare the project complete. Workers continued to clean up debris and finish the powerhouse roof, among other chores considered to be part of the mopping-up phase of construction. It was not until the morning of February 29, 1936, that Frank Crowe met with a government representative on the crest of the dam and officially turned over the job for their acceptance. In Washington, D.C., the next day, Secretary Ickes formally accepted the dam and the powerhouse on behalf of the government, terminating the contract exactly two years, one month, and twenty-eight days ahead of schedule. Hoover Dam was now officially finished.

Crowe, the star of the Boulder Dam Project and whose influence was the biggest reason that the construction finished ahead of schedule, collected not only his yearly salary of eighteen thousand dollars (a good amount in those Depression years) but also a bonus of 2.5 percent of Six Companies profit on the project. This amounted to approximately three hundred thousand dollars, which would have allowed him to retire comfortably. Crowe, however, chose to start work immediately on Parker Dam, 155 miles downstream from the Hoover Dam.

LAKE MEAD

The waters of the Colorado River slowly rose behind the new dam. At the bottom of the new reservoir were the remains of

Ragtown, one of the first encampments for those hoping to work on the Hoover Dam, as well as the vestiges of a thousand-year-old Indian pueblo. The reservoir would take six and a half years to fill completely. Once filled, the formerly muddy, brown waters of the Colorado River would be transformed into deep blues and emerald greens in the waters of Lake Mead. In 1936, Elwood Mead, a commissioner of the Bureau of Reclamation, died of a heart attack. Because he was such a strong advocate of the entire dam project, the decision was made to name the new reservoir Lake Mead in his honor.

It was soon recognized that Lake Mead, a new lake in the midst of a desert, would be an enormous recreational opportunity. The Bureau of Reclamation was reluctant to administer such a huge resource, and turned to the Department of the Interior for assistance. On October 3, 1936, the National Parks Service, part of the Department of the Interior, took over the

Jet skiers speed along Lake Mead. Today, Lake Mead offers a number of outdoor recreational activities.

management of the newly named Boulder Dam Recreational Area. This meant that Lake Mead was recognized as a national resource for outdoor recreation on the same scale as America's national parks. In 1964 President Lyndon Johnson expanded this area into a new Lake Mead National Recreation Area to include Lake Mohave, another man-made lake, and in 1974 a final expansion incorporated the Grand Canyon and these lakes into one extensive recreational area. Lake Mead has become a significant tourist attraction of its own, for boating, swimming, and camping, as well as fulfilling its original purpose of storing the waters of the Colorado River. Under the National Parks Service, the area would be supervised and maintained to preserve its quality for future generations.

THE FATE OF BOULDER CITY

Another issue that arose with the completion of the Hoover Dam was the fate of Boulder City, intended only as a temporary place to house the workers during construction. As workers were laid off and left for other projects, the population of the city shrank from seven thousand to four thousand, and by 1940 only twenty-six hundred people remained, most of them employees of the government or of the electric companies drawing power from the dam.

Six Companies's contract with the government had not only specified the building of Boulder City but its dismantling as well. Six Companies was supposed to remove all the temporary buildings it had erected, which would basically include most of the town's structures, except for the government administration buildings and residences. Six Companies made deals with demolition companies, selling them the various buildings to be demolished. These demolition companies would then take down the buildings and sell the salvaged lumber, wiring, plumbing, light fixtures, and other construction materials. The government did purchase two of the dormitories to house the workers in the Civilian Conservation Corps, who were building facilities for the new Boulder Dam National Recreational Area. Some of the workers' cottages were also sold to individuals who used them for tourist cabins, but much of the rest of Boulder City, including the mess hall, remaining dormitories, and hundreds of cottages, were destroyed.

However, the beginning of World War II and the arrival of the army to guard the dam saved Boulder City from complete destruction. Despite the prevailing opinion that Boulder City

This photo depicts an aerial view of contemporary Boulder City. Although scheduled to be dismantled once construction of the Hoover Dam was complete, Boulder City flourishes today.

would wither away and die, the city flourished as some of the former workers were allowed to buy their homes for one hundred to three hundred dollars and as tourism brought an increasing number of people to the area. Tourists came to see the dam, to visit the new recreation area around Lake Mead, and to gamble in the casinos of Las Vegas, which had gotten their start catering to the workers on the Hoover Dam. Hotels were built in Boulder City and along the highway into Las Vegas, and special excursion trains transported those who wanted to visit the dam.

Up until 1960, Boulder City continued to exist as a government-run reservation, a situation that the inhabitants of the city liked and wanted to maintain. Gambling and liquor were prohibited and the residents felt that the city was a safe area, protected from the outside world. Businesses, however, complained that the government limited growth, and the Bureau of Reclamation itself no longer wanted the task of administrating a city. It took

HOOVER DAM SECURITY

As an important American site both in terms of providing power and as a symbol of America, the Hoover Dam has always been considered vulnerable in times of national emergency. The Hoover Dam was considered a primary military target during World War II because it was a major source of electrical power for the defense industry in California. Companies there used Hoover Dam electricity in steel mills, aluminum plants, and aircraft plants, where sixty-two thousand airplanes were built for military purposes between 1941 and 1945. Shortly after the Japanese attack on Pearl Harbor in 1941, gun emplacements were built on the banks of Lake Mead by battalions of military police. These gun emplacements had six gun ports and were constantly manned. A single soldier remained in the gun emplacement at all times while a squad of riflemen were scattered in the rocks, twenty-four hours a day, in case of attack. Soldiers also guarded the dam itself and escorted all civilian vehicles across the dam. The gun emplacement on the Arizona side can still be seen today, built of steel and concrete and covered with local rock.

After September 11, 2001, and the attacks on New York City's World Trade Center and the Pentagon in Arlington, Virginia, the Hoover Dam was closed to all vehicle traffic because of the possibility of a terrorist threat there. Although restrictions have been relaxed somewhat since then, large commercial vehicles are still prohibited from the dam and must detour around it. Passenger cars, motor homes, and rental trucks may cross the dam after being inspected. If the inspectors cannot see completely within the vehicle because it is packed too full, that vehicle must also detour. Pedestrians are not allowed on the dam after dark, and cars are not allowed to stop. Hoover Dam is still important to the economy of the West, and has the potential for devastating consequences if it were to be damaged or destroyed and Lake Mead's waters were let loose.

fifteen years of struggle between the government and the residents of Boulder City before the Bureau of Reclamation was able to sign over control of the property. The city was finally incorporated in 1960. Boulder City today still prohibits gambling and restricts growth, resisting the urban sprawl of Las Vegas and making Boulder City some of the most expensive real estate in Nevada.

HOOVER DAM IN THE 1980s

The first real test of Hoover Dam as a method of flood control did not come until the flood of 1983, the result of heavy snowstorms in the Rocky Mountains that were followed by a heat wave and heavy rains. The runoff into the Colorado River between April and July was 210 percent above normal, and all the reservoirs along the Colorado began to fill. In early June water had to be released from Lake Powell behind the Glen Canyon Dam, and all this water came rushing down to Lake Mead. Author Joseph Stevens describes the situation:

> Late in the evening of July 2 [1983], the [Hoover] dam's giant steel drum gates were lifted and a foaming wave crashed into the spillway channels and was sucked into the diversion tunnels. A cloud of mist rose into the desert night, and after a hiatus of fifty-two years, the wild freight-train roar of the Colorado River was heard again in Black Canyon. The flood crested on July 24 when more than fifty thousand cubic feet of water per second was discharged through the diversion tunnels; the spill was continued until September 6, when the drum gates were closed. Millions of dollars' worth of damage occurred in the river corridor downstream from Hoover Dam, but the destruction was only a fraction of what it would have been if Lake Mead had not cut the peak from the flood.[30]

It was a tribute to the construction of the dam that so little damage was done to the diversion tunnels, despite water flowing through them at 120 miles per hour. Glen Canyon Dam, built in the late 1950s, suffered extensive damage to its diversion tunnels from the same flood, but Hoover Dam's diversion tunnels only suffered from slight pitting and scraping.

The 1980s also saw more important milestones in the life of Hoover Dam: the fiftieth anniversary of its construction in 1985, a new status as a National Historic Landmark, and the completion of the mortgage payments in 1987, when the costs of constructing the dam were finally paid off.

Currently, there are traffic concerns at Hoover Dam. United States Route 93 passes over the top of the dam, and the enormous congestion of business and tourist vehicles has created hazardous conditions. Every day thirty-five hundred pedestrians, ten thousand cars, and seventeen hundred trucks contribute to the congestion around the dam and interfere with daily dam operations. The construction of a bypass around the Hoover Dam area to alleviate these overcrowded traffic conditions and make the area safer is being studied.

ENVIRONMENTAL ISSUES AND HOOVER DAM

Although Hoover Dam continued to fulfill its original purpose, the environmental impact of the dam came under increasing scrutiny as America entered the twenty-first century. As early as 1977, the Bureau of Reclamation was already warning that the supply of water needed to irrigate the dry West could not be met indefinitely by the Colorado River alone. "The average annual water supply of the Colorado River is inadequate to meet compact allocations and treaty entitlements," it warned in a 1977 publication. "Deficiencies are expected to occur by year 2000. Competition for water will become increasingly severe for all uses, with many demands remaining unmet."[31] The Colorado River has become a succession of dams, reservoirs, and embankments, like a series of liquid steps reaching to the Gulf of California. This gulf, the river's historic outlet to the Pacific Ocean, has not actually been reached by river water since 1961, except during intermittent floods. It is estimated that every drop of Colorado River water has been used an average of three times by the time it dribbles to a trickle in the Mexican desert, and the water quality is declining.

Silt continues to be a problem as well. Silt had begun to accumulate in Lake Mead as soon as the gates of Hoover Dam were closed in 1935. As Philip Fradkin describes in his book *A River No More*: "The huge mud flats that were formed at the upper end of the reservoir reduced the storage capacity of Lake Mead by 137,000 acre-feet a year. Combined with a yearly evaporation loss of 800,000 acre-feet from Lake Mead, the effectiveness of the dam could be seen to have its limits."[32]

All these issues have caught the attention of various environmental groups, especially those who see dams as unnecessary intrusions on the natural life of rivers. The Sierra Club has been calling for the removal of dams from many rivers in the United States, claiming that dams inflict tremendous damage on fragile river ecosystems and that the amount of electricity generated by

COLORADO RIVER WATER SYSTEM

As soon as the Hoover Dam was built, work began on the other components of the planned water system of the Colorado River. The first major construction was the All-American Canal, named because it would run entirely on United States territory instead of dipping down into Mexico, as the original irrigation canals did in the first disastrous attempts to irrigate California's Imperial Valley. The All-American Canal cost $38,500,000. The money had been allocated from the Swing-Johnson bill that financed the Hoover Dam.

The All-American Canal originated at the Imperial Dam, which was built on the Colorado River near Yuma, Arizona. Its western end was connected to a desilting works, meant to remove silt from the river water through a series of six parallel settling basins. Huge trash racks would remove river debris from the water. Once the water had been cleaned of trash and silt, it was sluiced back into the river, and here the All-American Canal began: a concrete-lined ditch that roughly paralleled the river for several miles and then turned west, running into California's Imperial Valley for irrigation purposes. The canal was eighty miles in length, 130 feet wide at the bottom and 196 feet wide at water level. To prevent sand from blowing into the canal from the nearby sand dunes, they were sprayed with oil, and vegetation was planted along the canal to hold the sand down.

Today the complete water system on the Colorado River begins at the Grand Canyon, passes through the Glen Canyon Dam to Lake Mead, through the Hoover Dam and Davis Dam, through Lake Havasu to Parker Dam, Headgate Rock Dam, Palo Verde Diversion Dam, and Imperial Dam, before running into the All-American Canal and the newer Coachella Canal that runs 135 miles north past the Salton Sea. With the river water so completely controlled and regulated, it is hard to imagine the wild water that greeted John Wesley Powell on those first explorations in the 1860s.

these dams is not enough to make up for the human impact on the environment. The Sierra Club and other groups claim that the glut of oil and natural gas, and lower electricity costs, make hydroelectric power unnecessary. The organization American Rivers even posts a list on their website describing the ten ways that dams damage rivers. An unnamed member of the World Commission on Dams is quoted as saying, "When I visit a dam, I often find a plaque honoring by name the engineer, government leader, contracting firm and the height, size, date, volume of water held or diverted, power generated, [and] flood capacity measurements. And that's fine. But I don't find a plaque with the names of any species hurt, the names of any people displaced, the cost to taxpayers, the price of maintenance or decommissioning, or why this option was chosen over, say, windmills, solar panels, natural gas, groundwater pumping, demand management or some decentralized tools."[33]

Great dams such as the Hoover Dam are still being built worldwide, and they will continue to provide water management and energy for the needs of those countries. Future construction will have to be both environmentally responsible and socially acceptable, but as the world's population increases and its resources shrink, dams will continue to fulfill an important purpose.

Notes

Introduction

1. Quoted in Stephen Stept, WGBH Educational Foundation *The American Experience: Hoover Dam, The Making of a Monument*. PBS Home Video, 1999.

Chapter 1: From Idea to Construction

2. Quoted in Joseph E. Stevens, *Hoover Dam: An American Adventure*. Norman, OK: University of Oklahoma Press, 1988, p. 17.
3. Stevens, *Hoover Dam*, pp. 21–22.
4. U.S. Department of the Interior, Bureau of Reclamation, *Construction of Hoover Dam*. Las Vegas: KC Publications, 1976, p. 9.
5. Stevens, *Hoover Dam*, p. 33.
6. Quoted in Stevens, *Hoover Dam*, p. 121.

Chapter 2: Getting Started

7. Quoted in Andrew J. Dunar and Dennis McBride, *Building Hoover Dam: An Oral History of the Great Depression*. Reno: University of Nevada Press, 1993, p. 23.
8. Quoted in Al M. Rocca, *America's Master Dam Builder: The Engineering Genius of Frank T. Crowe*. New York: University Press of America, 2001, p. 208.
9. Quoted in Dunar and McBride, *Building Hoover Dam*, p. 50.

Chapter 3: The First Big Step

10. Dunar and McBride, *Building Hoover Dam*, p. 91.
11. Dunar and McBride, *Building Hoover Dam*, pp. 91–92.
12. Stevens, *Hoover Dam*, p. 104.
13. Rocca, *America's Master Dam Builder*, p. 239.

Chapter 4: Preparing the Riverbed

14. Quoted in Stevens, *Hoover Dam*, p. 174.
15. Frank Waters, *The Colorado (Rivers of America series)*. New York: Holt, Rinehart and Winston, 1974, pp. 347–48.

16. Stevens, *Hoover Dam*, p. 189.

17. U.S. Department of the Interior, *Construction of Hoover Dam*, pp. 17–18.

Chapter 5: Building the Dam

18. Stevens, *Hoover Dam*, p. 193.

19. U.S. Department of the Interior, *Construction of Hoover Dam*, p. 22.

20. Quoted in Dunar and McBride, *Building Hoover Dam*, p. 161.

21. Quoted in Stevens, *Hoover Dam*, p. 195.

22. Quoted in Dunar and McBride, *Building Hoover Dam*, pp. 267–68.

23. Quoted in Dunar and McBride, *Building Hoover Dam*, p. 268.

Chapter 6: The Final Touches

24. Julian Rhinehart, "The Grand Dam," *Nevada Magazine*, October 1995. www.usbr.gov/lc/hooverdam.

25. Quoted in Dunar and McBride, *Building Hoover Dam*, p. 282.

26. *Quoted in* U.S. Department of the Interior, Bureau of Reclamation, Hoover Dam, "Hoover Dam Sculptures and Star Map," p. 2. www.usbr.gov/lc/hooverdam.

27. Quoted in U.S. Department of the Interior, "Hoover Dam Sculptures and Star Map," p. 3.

28. Quoted in Stevens, *Hoover Dam*, p. 245.

29. Quoted in Stevens, *Hoover Dam*, p. 248.

30. Stevens, *Hoover Dam*, pp. 263–64.

31. Quoted in Philip L. Fradkin, *A River No More: The Colorado River and the West*. Berkeley, CA: University of California Press, 1996, p. 33.

32. Fradkin, *A River No More*, p. 182.

33. Quoted in American Rivers, "10 Ways Dams Damage Rivers," p. 3. www.americanrivers.org.

For Further Reading

Books

Craig A. Doherty and Katherine M. Doherty, *Hoover Dam*. Woodbridge, CT: Blackbirch Press, 1995. A wonderful overview of Hoover Dam's construction.

Luke S. Gabriel, *The Hoover Dam: A Monument of Ingenuity*. The Child's World, 2001. A simple and well-illustrated look at the dam construction.

Zane Grey, *Boulder Dam*. New York: Pocket Books, 1967. A fictional account of the workers on the Hoover (then called Boulder) Dam by a famous author of novels set in the American West.

David Macaulay, *Building Big*. Boston: Houghton Mifflin, 2000. A companion to the PBS series of the same name, this book has an excellent section on dam constructions, including details about the Hoover Dam.

Elizabeth Mann, *Hoover Dam*. New York: Mikaya Press, 2001. Contains illustrations and vintage photographs of the dam's construction.

James C. Maxon, *Lake Mead and Hoover Dam: The Story Behind the Scenery*. Las Vegas: KC Publications, 1980. Great modern photographs of Lake Mead and the Hoover Dam, with information about tourism and recreation.

Videotape

Judith Dwan Hallet, *Building Big: Dams*. Boston: WGBH Educational Foundation, 2000. Hosted by author David Macaulay, this video tells the story of the Hoover Dam's construction, as well as that of other dams around the world.

WORKS CONSULTED

Books

U.S. Department of the Interior, Bureau of Reclamation, *Construction of Hoover Dam*. Las Vegas: KC Publications, 1976. A reprint of an original government publication telling the story of the dam's construction.

Andrew J. Dunar and Dennis McBride, *Building Hoover Dam: An Oral History of the Great Depression*. Reno: University of Nevada Press, 1993. An excellent collection of original interviews with the people who actually built the dam.

Philip L. Fradkin, *A River No More: The Colorado River and the West*. Berkeley, CA: University of California Press, 1996. A modern, environmental view of the effects of man-made controls on the Colorado River.

J.W. Powell, *The Exploration of the Colorado River and Its Canyons*. 1895. Reprint, New York: Dover Editions, 1961. The firsthand account of John Wesley Powell's trips down the unexplored Colorado River.

Al M. Rocca, *America's Master Dam Builder: The Engineering Genius of Frank T. Crowe*. New York: University Press of America, 2001. The story of Frank Crowe's life.

Joseph E. Stevens, *Hoover Dam: An American Adventure*. Norman: University of Oklahoma Press, 1988. An excellent book telling the entire story of Hoover Dam's construction.

James Tobin, *Great Projects: The Epic Story of the Building of America, from the Taming of the Mississippi to the Invention of the Internet*. New York: Simon and Schuster, 2001. Contains a good overview of the Hoover Dam construction.

Barbara Vilander, *Hoover Dam: The Photographs of Ben Glaha*. Tucson: The University of Arizona Press, 1999. The story of Ben Glaha's photographs of Hoover Dam, illustrated with many of the actual photos.

Frank Waters, *The Colorado* (Rivers of America series). New York: Holt, Rinehart and Winston, 1974. A good description of the Colorado River and the building of the dam.

Donald E. Wolf, *Big Dams and Other Dreams: The Six Companies Story*. Norman: University of Oklahoma Press, 1996. Tells the entire story of Six Companies, during and after the Hoover Dam construction.

Videotape

Stephen Stept, WGBH Educational Foundation, *The American Experience: Hoover Dam, The Making of a Monument*. PBS Home Video, 1999. A sixty-minute video that chronicles the events and the people who built Hoover Dam, including interviews with workers and actual footage from the dam's construction.

Internet Sources

Shepherd Bliss, "Hoover Dam: Water Wars in the American West," 2002. TomPaine.commonsense, www.tompaine.com.

Julian Rhinehart, "The Grand Dam," *Nevada Magazine*, October 1995. www.usbr.gov/lc/hooverdam.

U.S. Department of the Interior, Bureau of Reclamation, Hoover Dam, "Hoover Dam Sculptures and Star map." www.usbr.gov/lc/hooverdam.

Websites

American Rivers , An organization dedicated to preserving America's rivers and strongly opposed to the presence of dams on rivers, including the Colorado. "10 Ways Dams Damage Rivers" www.americanrivers.org.

Public Broadcasting Service (www.pbs.org). Provides links to additional material from two PBS series relating to the Hoover Dam: David Macaulay's series *Building Big* (with an episode on dams) and the *American Experience* series (with an episode on Hoover Dam).

U.S. Department of the Interior, Bureau of Reclamation, Hoover Dam, National Historic Landmark. (www.usbr.gov). The government's website for everything related to the history of the Hoover Dam, including visitor information.

INDEX

rotors, 79

safety miner, 47
Salton Sea, 12, 99
Salton Sink, 12
Savage, Jack, 22
scabs, 39
scaffolding, 46–47
scrip, 58–59
Secret Service, 91
security, 96
September 11, 2001, attacks, 96
Sierra Club, 98–100
silt, 98
Six Companies
  accused of racism, 59–60
  asks Arizona to reduce workers' compensation, 65
  creation of, 26
  dam workers strike against, 37–39
  deadlines faced by, 43–44
  demolishing of Boulder City by, 94
  hires Crowe, 28
  problems between Ickes and, 58–60
  sues state of Nevada, 48
  turns over Hoover Dam to the government, 92
  wins contract to build Hoover Dam, 25
skip, 63
skip tender, 63
slump tests, 65–66
spiders, 81
spillways, 77–80
star map, 89
stators, 79

Stevens, Joseph E., 18, 39, 45, 51, 53, 64, 72, 97
strikes, 37–39
Swing, Phil, 20
Swing-Johnson bill, 20, 99

tar, 52
terrazzo floors, 87–89
Tierney, J.G., 75
Tierney, Patrick, 75
towers, 77–80
trash racks, 77
True, Allen, 87–89
tunnels, 27, 43–50, 78–80, 83–84
turbines, 79

Union Pacific Railroad, 22–23
Union Station, 31, 91
U.S. Army Air Force, 82
U.S. Bureau of Standards, 71
U.S. Department of Labor, 33
"Us Old Scabs on Boulder Dam" (parody), 39
Utah Construction Company, 26

Walter, Raymond, 22
Waters, Frank, 61–62
Wilbur, Ray Lyman, 23–24
Williams Jumbo (vehicle), 47
Williams, Woody, 47
Williamsville. See Ragtown
Winged Figures of the Republic, 89–90
Wobblies. See Industrial Workers of the World
World Commission on Dams, 99
World Trade Center, 96
World War II, 82, 94–96

Picture Credits

Cover Photo: © Lester Lefkowitz/CORBIS
© Associated Press/AP, 67, 73
© Bettmann/CORBIS, 21, 34, 40, 54, 57, 58, 70, 91
© Bureau of Reclamation, 19, 26, 46, 62, 81, 85, 87, 95
© CORBIS, 11, 12, 16
© Richard Cummins/CORBIS, 52
© Rick Doyle/CORBIS, 93
© Dave G. Houser/CORBIS, 90
© Hulton-Deutsch Collection/CORBIS, 31
© Brandy Noon, 76
© Schenectady Museum; Hall of Electrical History Foundation/
  CORBIS, 78
© Underwood & Underwood/CORBIS, 44

About the Author

Marcia Amidon Lüsted has a degree in English and secondary education, and has worked as a middle school English teacher, a musician, and a bookseller. She lives in Hancock, New Hampshire, with her husband and three sons.